HELLO SWEETHEART
...Get Me Rewrite

VAL SEARS

HELLO SWEETHEART
...Get Me Rewrite

Remembering the Great Newspaper Wars

KEY PORTER·BOOKS

Canadian Cataloguing in Publication Data

Sears, Val
   "Hello sweetheart, get me rewrite"

ISBN 1–55013–112–5

1. Reporters and reporting – Canada – History –
20th century. 2. Sears, Val. 3. Journalists –
Canada – Biography. I. Title.

PN4914.R5S42 1988   071'.1   C88–094282–7

Key Porter Books Limited
70 The Esplanade
Toronto, Ontario
Canada M5E 1R2

The publisher gratefully acknowledges the assistance of
the Ontario Arts Council.

Typesetting: Vellum Print & Graphic Services Inc.
Printed and Bound in Canada

88 89 90 91 92 6 5 4 3 2 1

Contents

For Meg
and the good times

Acknowledgments

Material for this book was drawn from personal recollections, interviews, private correspondence, newspaper files and remembered lies. In addition, the following books were helpful in reconstructing the period and events: *J.E. Atkinson of the Star* by Ross Harkness (Toronto: University of Toronto Press, 1963); *Bassett* by Maggie Siggins (Toronto: James Lorimer, 1979); *The Boyd Gang* by Marjorie Lamb and Barry Pearson (Toronto: Peter Martin, 1976); *Swim to Glory* by Ron McAllister (Toronto: McClelland and Stewart, 1954); *Fabian of the Yard* by Robert Fabian (London: The Naldrett Press, 1950); *In Court* by Jack Batten (Toronto: Macmillan, 1982); *Hurricane Hazel* by Betty Kennedy (Toronto: Macmillan, 1979); *Miracle at Springhill* by Leonard Lerner (New York: Holt, Rinehart and Winston, 1960); *Blood on the Coal* by Roger David Brown (Hantsport, N.S.: Lancelot Press, 1976); *Canadian Newspapers: The Inside Story* edited by Walter Stewart (Edmonton: Hurtig, 1980); *Paper Boy* by Stuart Keate (Toronto: Clarke Irwin, 1980); *News and the Southams* by Charles Bruce (Toronto: Macmillan, 1968); *Life in a Word Factory* by Ron Poulton (Toronto: Toronto Sun Publishing, 1976); Canada, Royal Commission on Newspapers, *Report* (Ottawa: Minister of Supply and Services, 1981).

1 | A Gentleman of Color

One summer morning in 1950 I was lying on a bench just inside the door of the Children's Aid Shelter in Vancouver, dealing with a hangover by moving as little as possible.

The reason I was there, suffering, was because of a seventeen-year-old girl from Montreal who was heir to a fortune of $2 million. She had disappeared, and I, along with several hundred other people, was looking for her.

Her name was Beverley Van Horne. She was very pretty, very rich and the great-granddaughter of Sir William Van Horne, who had built the Canadian Pacific Railway.

I was employed, at $30 a week, by the Canadian Press news agency in Vancouver as a rewrite man and occasional reporter. I had been instructed, as had employees of every other CP bureau in Canada, to find Miss Van Horne, intact or otherwise, and report upon her fate for the member papers of CP across the country.

It struck me that finding the missing teenager in Vancouver, when she had disappeared in Montreal, was unlikely. But, on a Monday morning, after a party weekend, it also seemed to me an inspiration to suggest I seek her at the Children's Aid Shelter where I could at least rest.

In time the director of the place arrived, roused me, and inquired what the hell I was doing sleeping on his bench.

I got groggily to my feet, followed him into his office, and asked if by any chance he knew the whereabouts of Miss Beverley Van Horne, late of Montreal.

He said no. I thanked him and made for the door.

"Wait a minute," he said. "Come back, I'll show you something."

He opened his desk drawer and it was stuffed with telegrams.

"These are from her family in Montreal, demanding I release her. She's in a cell in the back."

Oh Christ, can I see her? Can I talk to her?

No.

Will you tell me what happened, why she left, how she's been living, anything . . . please?

Yes.

When he was done I left in a taxi for the office—to hell with expenses, I'd use the streetcar ticket I'd been issued another time—and wrote the story.

It was carried in every newspaper in Canada and a good many in the United States.

It began: "Beverley Van Horne tried to scratch her name from Montreal's blue book when she ran away from school December 16 and became just another pretty teenager."

It was a clean beat. A scoop. A wonderful thing.

In all the tumbling years afterwards—in Toronto, and Washington and London, and Khabarovsk and Durban and Copenhagen and Tokyo and Dildo, Newfoundland—I never had another.

I have been a newspaperman all my life. A reporter in emergencies, but mostly a feature writer. A storyteller.

I knew that's what I wanted to be very early on, when I was a child in Vancouver and discovered Richard Halliburton. Halliburton is almost the best storyteller that ever was. An adventurer, he dived into a Mayan sacrificial well; bought a slave in Timbuctu; swam the Panama Canal, registered as the SS *Richard Halliburton*; flew about the world in his plane, "The Magic Carpet." And he wrote wonderful books about his travels. I wanted to be like him.

In high school I wrote a column called "By the Way " for the newspaper and was caught up in journalism for good. At the University of British Columbia I became managing editor of *The Ubyssey*, a college paper that produced a disproportionate number of professional writers after the war.

There was Pierre Berton, who has been yarning ever since, and Allan Fotheringham, the most delightful harvester of an anecdotal crop in the entire country. There was Jack Wasserman, a columnist of the glittering Vancouver night until his heart exploded at dinner and his ashes were inadvertently sent to the cleaners in a pallbearer's suit. There was Paul St. Pierre among the cowboys and Jack Scott and Ron Haggart and Marjorie Nichols and me.

Indeed, one of the jazziest writers was the sports editor, John Turner, who became prime minister of Canada.

It was a fine time for college newspapers, 1946; the war was just over, the campus was overflowing with veterans, battle-scarred and confident. For those of us from high school, never to be Spitfire pilots, it was a constant fight for attention. We had no war stories, we were just learning to drink, we did not have the sophistication of the men and women who had survived the battles of Halifax and Caen. So, we had to try harder, be wittier, cleverer, more world-weary, if we wanted to be part of the gang.

The Ubyssey, the college paper, was a real newspaper, published three times a week with real news of crime on campus, political debates, theater criticism, features. We were almost always in trouble with the authorities. But early on we learned what it is like to write under pressure, to wring the clichés out of our systems, to accept the flak for what we wrote, to experience the joy of writing a perfect sentence.

And we decided what kind of writing we wanted to do.

A reporter may be an investigator, an analyst, a researcher who prepares us for social change. He can preach, popularize, simplify, inform or advocate.

Or he may be simply a storyteller. Like me.

It is not the kind of newspapering that makes heroes. Those are the investigative reporters or war reporters. Men like Bob Woodward and Carl Bernstein of *The Washington Post* and the movie *All The President's Men*. Or Sidney Schanberg of *The New York Times* and *The Killing Fields*.

But storytelling, or, more properly, feature or color writing, is an honorable profession, and for many of us there is no other newspaper writing half so satisfying.

What the feature writer looks for are the oblique bits of stories, not only the anecdotes but the ironies.

I was in Ireland once, in Londonderry, standing in a doorway, listening to the handguns popping and the glass breaking, watching a young woman busy with her work on the opposite curb. I walked over to watch her stuffing Tampax tampons into beer bottles full of gasoline. The Tampax string made an excellent wick.

"What do you do when you're not making firebombs?" I asked.

"I teach nursery school," she said.

There are not many newspaper storytellers left in Canada. Editors like reporters. I don't know why. Maybe they never heard that the news was on television last night.

But there have been some who had a way with a

tale—Bruce Hutchison, Jack Scott and Pierre Berton in Vancouver; Val Werrier in Winnipeg; Jim Gray in Calgary; Gordon Sinclair and Gregory Clark in Toronto; Gratton O'Leary in Ottawa; Alden Nowlan in St. John. And there still are: Jamie Lamb out on the coast; E.K. Fulton, with Southams; Bob Lee and Roy MacGregor in Ottawa; Judy Steed and John Picton in Toronto; Hubie Bauch in Montreal; Alan Jeffers and Harry Bruce and Ray Guay in the Maritimes.

There is only one newspaper writer, of course: Joey Slinger at the *Star*.

The good ones, like some of these, usually go to work for magazines or become columnists. They can't write short or don't like editing or are busting with opinions. But columnists, even with their freedom, are kind of jealous of storytellers.

All across Canada, before journalism schools took over and homogenized the product, men and women brought a distinctive style to newspapers. Some were persuaders, the Jesuits of journalism; some revelled in the low life, writing the lavatorial reflections of a man with one hand free; others simply reported what they saw, what they heard, what they felt.

Through it all, the storytelling reporters, the feature writers, the color people hung on, increasingly shouldered to the inside by the investigators, the specialists, the hard-news, said-last-night journalists, OD'd on objectivity and their graffiti: the tedium is the message.

Even sports reporting got a whiff of the banal. In 1977, *Le Soleil's* Jean St. Hilaire—as reported by the Kent Commission on Newspapers—had this to say about sports journalism: "We have to get rid of the anecdotes, trite quotes and exaggerated images, and get into the sociological reality of sport. We must learn to assess events in terms of the effects they have on the life of society in general."

Jack McArthur, business columnist for *The Toronto Star*, said: "A newspaper, faced with the market as it stands, has two ways to go. One is to the interpretive, explanatory sort of reporting that requires immense amounts of knowledge, requires high priced people, requires time . . . the other is the pizzazz way . . . to hell with explanations; if you couldn't understand it, forget it."

I would argue they won't hear the interpretive, explanatory sermon unless they're in the tent. And it's pizzazz that beckons them in.

The feature writer must take his satisfactions where he finds them. Not for him—or more likely, her—the noble feeling of a villainy revealed, a junk bond explained, sexuality neatly categorized; voodoo economics exposed or free trade examined, exhumed and exhausted.

His stock-in-trade is the really neat lead. My personal favorite, written thirty years ago about a suicide I came upon in Vancouver, read: "Gertrude Kringle, always a tidy girl, hanged herself in the closet today."

Or the Chicago *Trib*'s recording of the death of the college-educated homosexual killer, Nathan Leopold, who was stabbed to death by a fellow prison inmate: "Nathan Leopold, for all his fine education, today ended his sentence with a proposition."

A feature writer can die happily with that on his record.

And for the publisher's bonus earned for an eight-part series called "Why Is My Daddy Unemployed?" writers will happily trade a vignette, an anecdote, a bit of gossip so delicious it melts in the mind.

Making up colorful stories is wrong, but it happens.

There is a man, still writing, who once did a piece for Fleet Street about Russians establishing bases on Canada's arctic ice cap. It was a doozer. He had flown low over the settlement but the Russkis had rolled oil drums onto the airstrip so he couldn't land. The hammer and sickle flew in the chill wind. But, oh my, he made the whole thing up as a *Daily Mail* man discovered when he arrived in the Yukon to hire the plane and get to the Reds. Harmless by Fleet Street standards perhaps. But embarrassing.

When I was very young I invented a story. It terrified me. I had been sent down to a prison in Rochester to interview a man who had posed as an English professor at a private boys' school in Toronto. He taught the toffs for years until he was caught. I forget why. He did come out to the warden's office when I asked to speak to him. But he wouldn't say a word, not a damn word.

I drove back to Toronto, convinced I was doomed. Money spent and no story. So, I made up the interview, witty, poignant, just as it might have been. The *Tely* used it and I sweated. But that was nothing compared to the next week when *Time* picked it up. Oh god, he's bound to see it. I'm finished.

But if the phoney professor did, he must have laughed, respecting a fellow con man, and never let on. I was saved. But never again, I swore.

Still, news stories can lie, can be plainly wrong. Even when they're right. And the color sometimes makes the difference. A man called Jenkins Lloyd Jones, then editor of *The Tulsa Tribune*, made the point nicely once in a lecture. He was dealing with the issue of whether papers are entitled to refer to a man's criminal record. But he made a larger point that truthtelling is an inexact science.

Consider, Jones suggested, these two stories:

"Mr. Gerald Cantonwine, 68, house painter, of 2273 E. 38th St., died yesterday in a Tulsa hospital after a long illness.

He was born in Danville, Ill., and came to Oklahoma in 1920. He is survived by his widow, Mrs. Mamie Cantonwine, prominent church worker."

Or:

"Death, which he had eluded in a dozen blazing gun battles, finally came yesterday to Jerry (The Gimp) Cantonwine, prominent early-day bank robber. The once-celebrated thief and gunman succumbed in a Tulsa hospital after a long illness. In 1922 Cantonwine, originally from Danville, Ill., was convicted of four bank robberies and a gold shipment theft. He served 15 years in McAlester penitentiary. On his release, he married 'Flaming Mamie' McGuire, his former look-out girl, and took up housepainting. The Cantonwines lived at 2273 E. 38th St. His widow is now the only survivor of a gang that once included Gaspipe Flynn, Brassknuckles O'Toole and Nitro Burke. She is a member of the Altar Guild at All Saints Church."

Long, long ago, when John Diefenbaker was alive and prime minister, he used to tell the story of how the Charter of the United Nations was first written on the back of a cigarette package in San Francisco and he had picked it up and kept it.

This wasn't just lace. It was nonsense.

The charter preamble, which is hundreds of words, was composed months before. American cigarette packages can't be written on. And Dief was a spectator high in the gallery when the preamble was first read.

I called him on it in a story and he blew up, threatening to sue me for calling him a liar. He was a great storyteller and I loved him for that at least. But he lied a lot.

To write color, to lie concealed in the bushes when friends of friends in high places tell stories about each other, you have to be equally embarrassing to all sides. No favorites. You have to be neutral, a human Switzerland.

With politicians or bankers on a spree or southpaw pitchers

or movie stars into a line or two of blow, there can be no mercy. Everything's on the record unless you agree it's off. And it's up to them to propose a deal, not you.

And you can become an embarrassment in front of your hard-news colleagues. If a press conference is really the only access to the family of the kid who has been stabbed in the school yard, you've got to ask Mom to describe the bedrom in detail, the toys she had, the books she read. This pisses people off. No matter, you'll be read for the color and you may even be able to slip in the message.

Most of my early schooling in these matters came at the feet of a wise old gnome, George (Pop) Finlay, the news editor of the CP bureau in Vancouver in the forties. My education there ended when I was fired for trying to organize a union.

This came as no real surprise because most of us in the bureau were au courant with head-office policy as we pried open the bureau chief's filing cabinet every night and read his correspondence. We did not like the bureau chief, who had been appointed as a reward for keeping the wire open in Winnipeg during the general strike. In fact, one of our wise guys would defecate regularly in the chief's private wash basin, and the chief's frustration at being unable to isolate the culprit with any known chemical test was a burden to him and a joy to us.

Prepared for dismissal, I graciously refused rehiring as a temporary summer replacement and began to clean out my desk. Then, in one of the twists of fate that inspire second-rate short-story writers, the world turned. Head office, namely Gillis Purcell, CP's God, bully and general manager, sent me a telegram that day, which read: "Feel you are making a mistake leaving CP. Please reconsider your resignation."

What in the hell was this? I quickly wired back collect: "Not resigning, fired. Send me my money."

God called me at home that night, suggesting a mistake had

been made. He didn't explain but I later concluded he had fired too many staffers for union activity—disguised as economy measures—and the courts might give him trouble.

I considered the matter deeply and wired again: "Will stay on if offered a job in Toronto and my train fare. 73s ['Regards' in our ancient telegraph talk]." A week later I was on my way to Toronto to look for gold in the streets.

I took a room at the Y with a chap who was an undertaking student and smelled awfully of formaldehyde.

My job, Purcell's revenge, was to work the graveyard shift, writing radio news and newspaper fillers—the short, factual sentences that were jammed in at the bottom of newspaper columns when the story ran out too short.

I made them up. Some of my favorites appeared in newspapers years later and I treasured stumbling upon one such as: "Polo fields in the Andes are 10 feet shorter than at ground level because the thin air is hard on the horses" or "Charlemagne was buried sitting upright on his horse" or a real inspiration for American papers: "In Kitty Hawk, North Carolina, the toast in the Kitty Hawk Inn is toasted exactly the same length of time as the first Wright brothers' flight." Go ahead, check it out. If you can find the Kitty Hawk Inn.

One morning, yawning and emptied of inspiration, I walked over to *The Telegram* and applied for a job. A month later, the managing editor, Doug MacFarlane, called me for an interview.

MacFarlane hired me. I was sent to the court and police bureau where Sinclair Stevens, someday to be in—and out of— the Mulroney cabinet, and I covered torso murders and alienation-of-affection cases. He was learning one trade, I another.

In time, I was rewarded by seeing a series I had written in

my off hours, about television coming to Toronto, appear on Page One.

MacFarlane called and said: "I guess you're ready. Start work in the editorial room tomorrow."

And so it began. Walter Stewart, later to be a grumpy author and even grumpier columnist, signed on about the same time. Years later he wrote: "*The Telegram* was a dreadful newspaper."

And he quoted a distinguished authority, me, as saying: "*The Telegram* was one paper that came with the garbage already wrapped in it."

I lied. It wasn't garbage. It was the fragrant leavings of contemporary history. It was the refuse of a battle between the *Star* and the *Tely* that consumed ten years of our lives, some of our loves, all of our skill. And oh what a lovely war.

2 | The Rivals

The newspaper publishers of the fifties—Don Cromie of the Vancouver *Sun*, Max Bell of *The Albertan*, Victor Sifton of *The Winnipeg Free Press*, Dick Malone of FP Publications Ltd., the Southam family of Ottawa and Montreal—were certainly powerful and frequently eccentric.

Stu Keate, who wrote about some of them in *Paper Boy*, recalls watching in astonishment as Bell, to prove his fitness to his editors, walked around his hotel room on his hands while large-denomination American bills fell out of his pocket.

But Toronto had something else again: Big John Bassett, publisher of *The Telegram* from 1952 until 1971, a man who owned a newspaper for the hell of it.

In his long and lively life, Bassett has really had only two big problems: sex and money. He's had a whole lot of both, of course, but even plenitude has its problems. Right now it was sex.

In 1967, during the long twilight of the paper, Bassett had stolen a woman away from another man. He wished to divorce his wife, Moira, who had given him three fine sons in nearly thirty years of marriage, and marry a beauty, twenty-four years younger and a reporter on the paper that he owned.

John White Hughes Bassett was fifty-two years old at the time, a big, powerful, wide-striding, high-rolling man, with piercing blue eyes that could make nuns and virgins wistful.

He was a sexy man, always had been, still is, and his wife, Moira, was a patient, forgiving, independent woman.

But now he had met Isabel Glenthorne Gordon, the wife of the son of an old friend, Crawford Gordon, who ran an airplane factory. Isabel was a teacher in North Hatley, the Bassett family's summer place in the Eastern Townships of Quebec. She came to work at the *Tely* as a reporter. In 1965, she won the Miss By-Line contest. Isabel and Big John fell passionately in love and Isabel left her husband, Crawford Gordon Junior, to join him.

"It was a helluva story," says Bassett now. "Here she was, going to marry this lecherous sonovabitch, a whole lot older than she was. She'd been married four or five years to this suitable young fellow. And I was a highly visible figure in Toronto."

What Bassett wanted to do was keep the whole messy business out of the paper—not hard to do with the one he owned, but *The Toronto Daily Star* was the problem. *The Globe and Mail*, in the morning, didn't much traffic in messy things. ("Women are raped, watchmen taped, girls into slavery sold. But you'll never read it in *The Globe and Mail* unless it's below the fold," members of the Press Club sang.)

The *Star*, Canada's largest newspaper, and the *Tely* had been battling each other viciously for half a century. By the sixties, the *Tely* was still trying to overtake the *Star*, but the combat was less poisonous than it had been a decade earlier.

Bassett decided to call the publisher of the *Star* and ask for a little cooperation.

Beland Honderich was a serious man; a quiet man; a tough, unforgiving man. He was a man who would ultimately destroy the *Tely* and pay $10 million for its bones, the circulation list.

He came from a Mennonite family and worked his way up through the *Star*'s ranks with talent and determination. During the gaudy days of the fifties, he was far away from the gore, acting as financial editor and editor of the editorial page.

When he became publisher of the *Star* in 1961, it turned gray and—because he recognized that the razzmatazz days were over and Bassett did not—became very, very successful.

But this day in 1967, Honderich also had a problem. He, too, was getting a divorce. And Bassett knew it.

"Honderich was practically unknown as far as the general public was concerned," says Bassett. "He was a very shy man. I called him and said: 'Bee, I want to make a deal with you. If you guarantee there'll be nothing in the *Star* about my divorce, I'll give you the same guarantee: there'll be nothing about yours in the *Tely*.' He agreed immediately. He was horrified by any publicity. In fact, the public wouldn't have given a damn about his divorce. I sure got the best of that deal."

It was one of the few times the two publishers would find a common ground in their long rivalry. And what was little more than the casual exercise of power for Bassett must have been disturbing for Honderich. For as much as he loved privacy, his ethics were rigid and the decision to use his paper for a personal purpose would not have been made lightly. Today he has put the entire incident out of his mind.

The two men could not have been more different.

Bassett embraced everything—deals, women, politics, his sons, the passing years—with a beaming zest.

In the sixties, he was busy with the Argo football team, Maple Leaf Gardens, television, while, slowly, behind him, the *Tely* was dying.

But goddamn, he says now, his mind unreeling back to the

fifties, that was *the* time—"a marvelous time, just a wonderful time."

Since the beginning—when the *Star* was founded by twenty-one striking printers and two apprentices in 1892 and took on John Ross Robertson's solidly entrenched *Evening Telegram*—it had been war: vicious, unforgiving, bigoted, battling.

Canada has been a newspaper battleground, of course, for a century, and the corpses of defeated papers yellowed in the files.

But the pace has been particularly deadly since World War Two, so much so that the Royal Commission on Newspapers was established by the Liberal government in 1980 to look at the whole business of death and mergers.

The Vancouver *Sun* and *The Province*, said historian Charles Bruce, "treated Vancouver readers to some of the liveliest cut-and-thrust of modern times."

But in 1946 a strike at *The Province*, long and bitter, crippled it and, in 1946, a new company, Pacific Press, was formed to publish both papers. Columnist Scott Young of *The Globe and Mail* wrote: "Each paper has assured its readers that it will retain its former character. Since the chief characteristic of each paper was its bitter competitive spirit toward the other, this character-retention will be quite a trick, something like watching a wrestling match between Siamese twins."

The twins are still wrestling out on the coast but nobody much cares.

In Edmonton, the *Journal* and the *Bulletin* were at merry odds for years, occasionally on curious fronts.

In 1947, they had a bench war. The *Journal* had been setting out benches all over town bearing the slogan "Rest and Read *The Journal*." The *Bulletin* attacked with a forest of their own benches. The citizens of Edmonton had more room to sit than they had to walk.

But it was no good. On January 20, 1951, the *Bulletin* carried an eight-column head: THE BULLETIN ENDS PUBLICATION TODAY.

In Winnipeg, the *Tribune*, cocky enemy of the *Free Press* for half a century, finally died at its feet, beaten by strikes and *Free Press* money. And, in Ottawa, the *Journal*, sober rival of the *Citizen*, was killed and the venerable *Montreal Star* failed to survive a strike which *The Gazette* managed to avoid.

No newspaper struggle, however, could match the thump and clang of the battle between the *Star* and the *Tely*.

The *Telegram* was imperial and blindly Conservative. The *Star* and its owner, J.E. Atkinson, in the *Tely's* view, was Liberal and, indeed, "Bolshevic."

Day after day, says Atkinson's biographer, Ross Harkness, "Mr. Atkinson was pictured to readers of the *Telegram* as an evil old man, hunched in his office spinning Machiavellian plots for the destruction of the Empire, Protestantism and Western civilization."

Atkinson, "Holy Joe" to most Torontonians, was mostly indifferent to Robertson's furious campaigns. He had a formula for the *Star*, which the *Tely* did not catch up with until the fifties, when it nearly worked for them.

Far from being holy, it was a combination of sex and sensation:

Come fill up our columns with sob stuff and sex
Shed tears by the gallons and slush by the pecks.
Let the presses revolve like the mill-tails of hell
For Jesus and Dickens and Edith Cavell.

The Press Club doggerelists of 1934 had it about right: the

Star was filled with sex, serials and religious soap operas. The *Tely*, for curious reasons, preferred Orange parades, Ukrainian weddings and bile.

By 1950, the *Tely* had been bought by George McCullagh—a wealthy dealmaker, owner of *The Globe and Mail* and friend of the Bassetts—for $3,610,000. The *Star*, after Holy Joe's death, had passed into the hands of trustees, with profits to go to the Atkinson Charitable Foundation.

The *Star*'s president was H.C. Hindmarsh, the dreaded "H.C.H." in his memos, a tough bird whose hand was everywhere in the paper. He probably managed a thin smile when he heard what McCullagh had done.

"The outstanding thing that brought me into the evening-newspaper field was to knock off the *Star*," McCullagh told a mass meeting of *Telegram* employees the day after he bought the paper. "The *Star* has done enough to the profession of journalism that we ought to go in and teach it a lesson. . . . I'm going to knock that shitrag right off its pedestal."

To lead the destruction, McCullagh called his young pal, John Bassett, who had bought the Sherbrooke *Record* and was busy running it. He asked him to be advertising manager—although actually to run things. "When can you come?" McCullagh asked. "Is tomorrow too soon?" replied the delighted Bassett. By the end of the week he was in Toronto.

"I really thought we could catch the *Star*," recalls Bassett. "But the *Tely* was a mess. I had no idea before I came how bad it was. And McCullagh had no idea what he had bought. The circulation manager couldn't even give me the circulation figures. The whole thing was a facade."

The *Tely* building was a baroque, brick monument on Melinda Street, just down from the corner of King and Bay, the center of Toronto's financial world. If you didn't want to take the creaking elevator up to the editorial floor, you could climb a twisting iron staircase that rose up out of the tiny lobby's tile floor.

Downstairs there were three underground sublevels where the big Hoe presses thundered and shook. The pressmen called it "The Black Hole." A steady stream of debris rained down on them through the iron-mesh floors. There were six presses, but they couldn't be run all at once and the most they could print was forty-eight pages. There were no color pictures although the final edition each day was printed on pink paper.

Upstairs, the editorial room was a set from *The Front Page*—wooden desks piled high with papers, tubes clattering overhead, filthy windows, poor light. At one point, the city desk had a bell to be rung to signal the approaching deadline, but passers-by kept punching it, and it lost its urgency. In any case, it wasn't as bad as the Vancouver *Sun*, where Musak had been installed and the selections were speeded up as deadline approached. In the last seconds before the editions went to press, reporters were madly trying to keep time with Rossini's overture to, among others, "The Lone Ranger."

The *Tely* was called "The Old Lady of Melinda Street."

A few blocks northwest, on King, the *Star* had built a twenty-three-story, $4-million tower in 1929 that was cleaner, neater and far more efficient than its rival. The *Star* had six modern presses and could print up to eighty pages.

Along with Bassett, McCullagh sent another man to the *Tely*. He was the *Globe's* city editor, Doug MacFarlane, the man who would general the *Tely* troops all through the fifties and into the sixties, until Bassett fired him.

Doug MacFarlane was like Walter Burns, the conniving, magnificent managing editor of *The Examiner*, in *The Front Page*. He also looked like another newspaperman, Clark Kent, six-foot-two with shoulders to match. He inspired in reporters an equal mixture of fear and worship. MacFarlane had been editor of the *Maple Leaf*, the Canadian Armed Forces paper overseas in World War Two, until he was fired at the end for criticizing the brass.

"McCullagh had taken a fancy to me at the *Globe*," MacFarlane recalls. "He felt I was putting some sparkle and life into the *Globe*, and the *Tely* was much in need of a similar approach. I agreed to go if he would make me city editor and pay me as managing editor. He said okay, so I went."

Over at the *Star*, the Rommel to MacFarlane's Patton would be a gentle journalist and probably the finest editor the *Star* ever had. His name was Borden Spears. He was soft-spoken, brilliant—a gold-medallist in history from the University of Western Ontario—and a man dedicated to the job of journalism.

In later years, a biographer recalls, Spears was sometimes embarrassed to speak of the excitable, and sometimes gaudy journalism of the fifties. He once recalled, "I knew at the time what we were doing wasn't respectable. But it was so much goddam fun."

In his last years, he was the *Star*'s ombudsman and was senior consultant to the Royal Commission on Newspapers. When he died, I wrote that Spears "brought the zest and experience of a lifetime in the newspaper business that began with chasing ambulances and wound up with chasing errors and journalistic responsibility. In between, there has been a bookful of adventures, of editorial ups and downs, a few regrets, but mostly of good times with good people who transformed Toronto journalism from sensationalism to grown-up responsibility and a new kind of excitement."

When Bassett arrived at the *Tely* and got the circulation more or less sorted out, it was just over 200,000. The *Star*'s was just over 400,000. It was a huge gap to bridge, but McCullagh was breathing fire.

"The smart talk will soon be about the waning *Star*," he snarled to *Time* magazine. "That fellow Hindmarsh is so ugly that if he ever bit himself he'd get hydrophobia."

Bassett read the magazine and was appalled. McCullagh apparently didn't understand that Hindmarsh held a card that could fold the *Tely* overnight.

"I went up to George's farm that night and he said, 'Have you seen *Time* today?' I said 'Oh, yes, I've seen it.'

"'That was a great crack you made. But do you know what I'd do tomorrow if I was Harry Hindmarsh? I'd put the *Tely* out of business. Don't you know that during the war, in order to conserve manpower, the *Star* and the *Tely* had carrier boys carrying both papers. Every boy that carries the *Star* carries the *Tely*. What do you think would happen next Monday if Hindmarsh said to his circulation manager: No kid carrying the *Star* and *The Star Weekly* can carry the *Tely*. He could take his choice. You'd have no carrier boys.'

"George went white. He was shocked. Then he said, 'Look, I tell you what you do. You make an appointment with Hindmarsh, be very polite, call him sir and all that . . . speak about your father . . . ease the situation . . . tell him maybe we ought to separate the carriers now.'"

Bassett got an appointment. H.C.H. couldn't have been nicer or more friendly, he recalls, and in an orderly way, over the months, the *Tely* built up its own carrier system.

As the decade began, Canada—and particularly Toronto —was ready for some excitement. People were making money, particularly in real estate. A widow sold a sixty-five-acre farm just outside of Toronto for $145,000, only to see it sold for $395,000 a year later. Reporters at the *Tely* could walk across the street to the Stock Exchange and make lunch money buying and selling in a half-hour.

Suddenly advertising exploded. New agencies seemed to be

opening every week, recruiting newspapermen. When they couldn't recruit, they simply hired by the hour. One afternoon, I got a call at the *Tely* from a friend in an agency who wailed: "Val, we're stuck for ideas. Come over and help. We're filming a bread commercial and it's dying."

I got a taxi over, sat in a director's chair and ordered more balloons.

"Quick," flunkies yelled, "more balloons! Mr. Sears wants more balloons!" I ordered the cameras to film a little, golden-haired girl holding a loaf of bread, dancing among the balloons. Great. They gave me 200 bucks. Was I in the wrong business?

Sixty-six percent of car owners paid cash for their automobiles and you could get a Persian-lamb coat for $387 during the fifties. Canada's gross national product rose from $18.4 billion to $36.8 billion. In that decade more than a million immigrants arrived. Toronto was adding 50,000 new residents a year.

Maybe Canadians were ready for the Boyd Gang and Fabian of the Yard and Marilyn Bell and the rest of the adventures the *Tely* was soon to offer because we were so goddamn dull. Or so George Ferguson, the editor of *The Montreal Star*, told a New York audience: "We behave ourselves and have a tradition of law and order which surpasses yours. . . . Our divorce rate is much lower than yours, we stay much at home, we go to church on Sundays in surprisingly large numbers, and, taken all round, we are a respectable lot—respectable, but inclined to be dull. Our virtues and our vices alike are pedestrian. We lack vividness and color and violent emotion. . . . "

So, when a pretty little girl started swimming across eel-spawning Lake Ontario . . . or a bunch of miners in Nova Scotia were trapped underground until a pipe reached them and the rescuers could hear their hymns . . . folks were ready for some secondhand excitement, at least.

The *Tely* and the *Star* were happy to ride the wave. Or, when necessary, to create it.

When MacFarlane arrived to take on the *Star*, he and Bassett reckoned their best chance was with a combination of aggressive news coverage and promotion.

"We had caught the *Star* in a period of doldrums," says MacFarlane. "H.C.H. wasn't very well, the editors were changing. We caught them with their guard down. In the first six months we gained about 60,000 circulation."

MacFarlane inherited an editorial staff of steady veterans but he also began to bring in new men, a lot of them Brits, who arrived at Union Station with their cardboard suitcases, all claiming to be Fleet Street veterans. And some of them were.

Bassett, meanwhile, had bought the *Tely*.

His old friend George McCullagh, sick and depressed, was found on an August day in 1952, drowned in his swimming pool. Some said an accident, some said not. He was forty-seven.

Backed by department-store millionaire John David Eaton, who guaranteed a bank note of $4.25 million, and with the Sherbrooke *Record* as collateral, Bassett swung the deal. The next-highest bidder was William Loeb, the ultra-right-wing publisher of New Hampshire's *The Manchester Union*. Loeb told me years later that had he won, he would have come to Canada and taken out Canadian citizenship. It would have been a very different *Tely* under Loeb. He was loony.

Once, when some employees came to him with a grievance, he invited them into his office and, while they sat down, drew his revolver and shot the office cat—"Now, gentlemen," he said to the dumbstruck printers, "what can I do for you?"

Bassett's deal was a complex one, designed to intertwine the two families and offset the damage of succession duties. The shares would be held in trust for the four Eaton sons and the three Bassett children.

"My signature on the bank note was worth nothing," says Bassett, "but it was countersigned by John David Eaton, which was worth plenty, and the banks took great comfort from that."

As soon as he had control, Bassett began to interest himself and the paper in Toronto's theater scene. While MacFarlane was hiring reporters, Bassett was signing up columnists and critics.

"Entertainment pages didn't really exist in those days. I got Nathan Cohen started on the *Tely*. I hired Mavor Moore. Nathan was very cross. 'Nathan,' I said, 'the theater in Toronto is a very delicate flower and you're too tough, you'll kill it. It isn't strong enough to sustain you on a regular basis.' Nathan went to the *Star*. Then Mavor Moore was the big man, until he got bored and quit. The *Globe* stole [Herbert] Whittaker from *The Gazette*. That's how all the entertainment pages got started.

"We began the Op Ed page and the Action Line page, as well. We'd start something and the *Star* would copy it."

Bassett was into everything at the *Tely*. He began to create his own legend. One famous day, recorded in every tale of the *Tely*, he found a story in the *Star* that was not in his paper. He summoned his editors and delivered a long tirade about their incompetence and stupidity.

When he paused for breath, MacFarlane said quietly: "The reason that story isn't in *The Telegram* today is that we had it yesterday."

Bassett never missed a beat but smiled and said: "Gentlemen, happiness is a day when you find the publisher is full of shit."

Over at the *Star*, as *Tely* circulation began to climb, there was a slight feeling of unease—no real concern, but unease. Leading newspapers could be killed by second-raters, particularly if there were strikes—the Vancouver *Sun* had destroyed the strikebound *Province* and, years later, *The Montreal Star*, also struck, succumbed to *The Gazette*. For the first time in many years, wrote Ross Harkness, the *Star* was faced with competition that was as intelligently directed as it was aggressive.

But as 1950 began, the *Star* had forged ahead in an area that, in the end, was to defeat all the *Tely*'s editorial innovation: classified ads.

Once, the *Tely* had been advertised as "the paper with the want ads." Now, the *Star* was publishing more classifieds than the other two Toronto papers combined.

But Bassett and MacFarlane were undaunted. "I was young, I was optimistic," says Big John. "John David Eaton couldn't have cared less what was happening. He had great confidence in me. What the hell, I was a news guy, all the publishers were news guys. Not like now. Some of them are bookkeepers. We thought in news terms. Our people had a tremendous feeling of loyalty to the *Tely*. They were all paid a good deal less than the *Star* guys were paid. The odd thing was that the *Star*, through the years, had the best working conditions, time off, certainly wages. But most people didn't like working there. I don't know why. Nobody wanted to work on the Toronto *Star*. We never had trouble getting people from the *Star* and they came for less money."

MacFarlane was building a news team of steady, experienced, reliable reporters and a new bunch of young men and women, excited by the prospect of taking on the *Star* and making a name for themselves in Big Town.

It would be ten years later before the *Star* had a team to match it, although by 1960, under Honderich, the *Star* had put together what was probably the most talented group of men and women ever assembled on a Canadian newspaper—Pierre Berton, Peter Newman, Ron Haggart, Bob Fulford, cartoonist Duncan Macpherson, Lotta Dempsey, Charles Templeton, Ralph Allen, Jeannine Locke, a remarkable collection of egos and expertise that did not, could not, last.

But as the fifties began, the *Tely* newsroom was a scratching, restless place, everybody clamoring for a chance at Page One and not too particular how they got there.

The pay was low—new reporters started at $45 a week—but there were compensations that the morality of the seventies and eighties forbids—free rail passes from the kindly PRs on the railway, vacations in Bermuda in return for a travel-page piece, liquor at Christmas and, up at the provincial legislature, a personal "stationery allowance" from the government and a chance to serve as paid secretary to an obscure government commission. It was corruption, thin but wide.

Along with the steady men and women—Allan Kent, Dorothy Howarth, Ron Poulton—were some quite astonishing eccentrics.

Eddie Palmer on the night desk. What was curious about Eddie, a one-legged former merchant seaman, was that he ate glass. It was unnerving for new people to glance up and see Eddie editing and chewing moodily on a flashbulb or a tumbler, swallowing without a hiccup.

Once, at a party, a man in the apartment above Eddie's came down to complain about the noise. Eddie answered the door and faced the complainant, who was wearing pajamas and, fatally, rimless glasses. Eddie pulled him slowly forward and ate his lenses, first one and then the other. The complainant fled, shrieking. Naturally he called the police. Certain explanations, promises and a drink or two were necessary for the understanding and publicity-conscious officers.

Or John MacLean, a legend even afterwards. MacLean, fine photographer and a good reporter, was also completely oblivious to the parameters of acceptable behavior. One night, while making bergoo, a sort of liquid stew he favored, he was unnerved by a radio playing in the apartment below. So, John bored a hole in the living-room floor with a large brace and bit, while his dinner guests waited. He then poured a bowl of bergoo down the hole and, presumably, onto the offending radio below. We had barely got to dessert when the police arrived.

At the time of the Suez crisis, MacLean, carrying a large bag of sandwiches, stowed away in the chain locker of the Canadian aircraft carrier *Magnificent*, ready to sail with it to Suez and report on events. Unhappily, he was caught.

Many were at the *Tely* to prepare themselves for other careers, some for greatness. Charles Taylor, son of billionaire E.P. Taylor, was hired without checking his paternal references. One night, finding a flaw in a story he had filed, I called the number listed for his house, asked for Charles and was informed in a cultured voice: "The young master is at dinner and cannot be disturbed." I did not find the joke amusing and snarled that the goddamn young master better get his ass to this phone or he'd be out of a job tomorrow and would likely starve. Charles came to the phone with an explanation about the family butler. I was awestruck by a sudden vision of endless beer for our parties.

The labor reporter became a provincial cabinet minister, another went on to be press secretary to Mike Pearson and Pierre Trudeau. Several, including the chief police reporter, became millionaires by founding another newspaper when the *Tely* folded. Some, bereft of talent, ended up in television.

The women reporters were a generation away from the feminist commandoes of the sixties, so bewitchingly described by Heather Robertson in *Canadian Newspapers: The Inside Story*, one of them on *The Winnipeg Tribune*:

> We were different from the newspaperwomen who had preceded us. We had no tits. It had been customary to measure the talent of female staff members at the *Tribune* by the size of their bra cups; the Women's editor was a statuesque 38D, columnist Ann Henry was a stunning 36 Triple C. We were all As. We were different in other ways, too. . . . We preferred money to compliments. We preferred a good book to a dull party. We were cool, university-educated daughters of the middle class, confident, ambitious, tougher in many ways than the terrible men, most of whom were grizzly bears with bunny-rabbit hearts. Refugees from marriage and the tedious female professions of schoolteaching and social work, we weren't there because we needed a job, or knew how to type or even because we wanted to write: we were looking for excitement, independence, power. We were the first of the formidable feminists.

The *Tely* and *Star* women were wily, proto-feminists who could steal a picture, vamp a cop, slug a rival or stitch a wound, entirely unaware that they were exploited and that the militant sisterhood was on the way to rescue them.

The *Tely* woman's editor dressed like an unmade bed, yet she was feared in the fashion world and her pages reflected some of the good common sense that had distinguished Madge Merton of the *Star*, generations earlier. Madge, it is recorded, could comfort an overweight woman of the 1900s: "Some human beings are stout, just as some dogs and some horses and cows are heavily built. You must not find fault with your nature. If your digestion is good and you take sufficient exercise, I wouldn't worry about it, if I were you."

So much for Jane Fonda.

Among the best of the *Tely* reporters, certainly the most dapper and precise, was Allan Kent. But even he could occasionally be ruffled.

In 1955 when Newfoundland premier Joey Smallwood had hired a Latvian, Dr. Alfred Valdmanis, to be the island's economic czar, the *Star's* Jack Brehl had managed an exclusive interview with Alfred.

Allan was told to get one, as well. He called a friend, Stu McLeod, Canadian Press in St. John's and a buddy of Smallwood's, and asked if he could arrange something. Smallwood was extremely reluctant because the *Tely* had been dumping on him for hiring the Latvian.

When Kent got back from Newfoundland, he was shaking his head.

"When I got to the airport in St. John's," he said, "Smallwood met me in a limousine. There was a sheep in the back seat. He never said a word and we drove to his farm. When we got there, he led me through the yard to the chicken house and we climbed up a ladder to the loft. The chickens squawked but Smallwood never said a thing.

"Finally, as we crouched in the chickenloft, he turned to me and said: 'The reason you're interviewing me here, Kent, is because the *Tely* is chickenshit.'"

Over at the *Star*, during the fifties, the reporters may have been more sensible but the stories were zanier. Some of the best, the readers never got to read.

Take the Great Polar Basin Expedition. They don't do polar expeditions like that any more.

It was a project to set a fifty-year-old redheaded woman

down at the North Pole, the first female to accomplish such a thing. *Star* reporter George Bryant heard about the plan while doing a story on the Explorers' Club in New York and immediately signed the *Star* aboard. The woman, whose name was Peggy, was the wife of a U.S. airforce colonel who used to be in the Mounties.

From the beginning there were difficulties. First, Peggy and her husband were not speaking, so they communicated with notes. Then, there was money. The pair had managed to get some frozen-food companies to donate supplies, but when the money ran low they ate up the goodies in New York.

Then the colonel, resurrecting an ancient DC-3 that had been rusting in the California sun, flew up to Chesterfield Inlet on a reconnaissance run, taking an increasingly dubious Bryant with him. The crew of the flying wreck ran up such a bill at the Hudson's Bay Company they had to flee back to New Jersey.

The *Star*, meanwhile, had sent another reporter, Buck Johnston, to New York where he was supposed to man a radio and write Peggy's day-to-day adventures as she neared the Pole. A sled was constructed in a Brooklyn garage and a New Hampshire clergyman who raised huskies had his team recruited.

As Day One approached—and the *Star* in Toronto prepared a huge picture layout headed STAR TAKES OFF ON POLAR EXPEDITION—Peggy and the bunch scraped together their final suppplies, a barber pole to be planted on the Arctic spot and a case of champagne. They persuaded the clergyman to accompany them in lieu of payment. The plane was loaded, including a now thoroughly frightened Bryant, while Johnston climbed up the Teterboro control tower to report the takeoff and signal editor Borden Spears in Toronto that the presses could roll with the story.

"Have they gone, can we go with the story?" shouted Spears over the phone to Johnston.

"Oh, they've gone," said Johnston, morosely, "but you'd better hang on. They didn't have room for the dogs."

After several days at Goose Bay and beyond—with Bryant spending one night in an igloo with a polar bear sniffing around outside—Peggy passed a note to her husband suggesting they withdraw back to New Jersey.

Star readers never did learn what happened to the Great Polar Basin Expedition.

Bryant, undismayed, immediately organized another foray, this time to meet a stone-age tribe in the Amazon. This time he wisely did not go along. Reporter-photographer Doug Blanchard was assigned.

When he returned, after some weeks, Buck Johnston asked him how he had got along with stone-age Indians who had never seen a white man before.

"Stone-age, hell," said Blanchard, "I had to pay them a hundred dollars each before they would take their clothes off."

With the death of *The Star Weekly*, the newspaper's weekly magazine, such expeditions became a rarity. But curious tales —many never printed—remain hidden in the stacks of every newspaper. When I worked for the *Star* in later years, there was the Great Chinese Bomb Scare.

I was in Washington as correspondent and one day got a call from the national editor, whispering, breathless with excitement, "Get on a plane and get to Toronto right away. We've got a story so big I don't dare tell you about it on the phone. The CIA may be listening."

Wow.

I grabbed a taxi to Baltimore airport, flew to Toronto and raced into the office. The editor—now the respected head of a journalism school—whipped me into his office, shut the door and handed me some papers. They were photostats of letters, reduced in size by a copying machine. One bore the White House crest, another the "seeing eye" logo of the Central Intelligence Agency, another the mark of the U.S. State Department, still another an army brigade headquarters emblem. They were signed by the president of the United States, John Kennedy, the CIA chief, a general or two, and seemed unmistakably authentic, down to the secretary's initials.

Together they outlined and authorized an incredible plot —nothing less than the planting of a ring of hydrogen bombs around the mainland of China, undersea and underground. China was then to be warned that the cataclysmic boundary existed and that, if she ever threatened war against the West, they would be set off. The plot was called "Operation Expensive Place."

I was stunned and frightened at the same time. "Take those letters back to Washington," the editor said, "and authenticate them. As soon as you can, write it."

"Where did these come from?" I asked.

"Two kids on a bus in Toronto saw them fall from a man's briefcase when he got off," he said. "They picked them up and brought them in to us. I phoned the number on the CIA letter and it's the CIA's Langley headquarters all right."

In Washington the next day, I tore off the CIA and White House crests, photostated them and set off to Virginia. The spooks at Langley said the crest looked like theirs. There were some differences, but nothing major. Where had I got it? I mumbled something and left. The White House said their crest was authentic.

I walked back to the office in a daze. A scoop. The goddamn biggest scoop the world had ever seen. Bigger even than my finding Beverley Van Horne. I sat down in the office, trying to figure how to write it. The name "Expensive Place" bothered me. I thought some more. Then I remembered. Some time back I had read a spy novel by Len Deighton, called *An Expensive Place to Die*. It was about a plot to ring mainland China with bombs. . . . Shit.

I called the library and got the number of Deighton's American publishing house. I called them in New York. By any chance . . .

"Oh, sure," said the helpful lady, "when the book came out in hardcover we had some phoney letters printed that were part of the plot and put them in a pouch inside the front jacket. Good promotion, we thought. But it was too costly so we dropped it after a few books."

My God. I sweated. Supposing I'd written it. I called the editor.

"Yes, yes," he said, "does it check out?" No, I said, and explained. There was a silence in Toronto. "Don't ever tell this story," he said and hung up.

I walked down the hall and stuffed the letters under the office door of *The Globe and Mail* correspondent. I hoped he didn't read spy stories. He didn't.

In the fifties, *Star* and *Tely* reporters were heavily armed for these adventures, an Underwood portable and a 4 × 5 Speed Graphic camera. The Speed Graphic was particularly handy for thumping rivals in the usual melees. A big black box, with bellows and a flashgun, it weighed about seven pounds, loaded.

Ads for the thing said: "The Speed Graphic is so intimately associated with the work of the press that it has almost become a symbol for a reporter. An amateur equipped with a Speed Graphic and a flash outfit is even frequently admitted within police and fire lines."

The flashbulbs had many uses. They could, for instance, be used to illuminate the subject at night. But the small ones, thrown into a fireplace at a party, offered a dandy flash and explosion. And the big, powerful ones, screwed into a light fixture, would explode with a blinding, mind-numbing brilliance when an unsuspecting outsider flipped the switch.

Photographs were facts but both papers put a little spin on stories from time to time. The *Star*, during this period, before it and today, did not and does not consider objectivity a virtue.

"The newspaper stood for certain things," wrote Ross Harkness, "and it stood for them in every column from the weather on page one to Eaton's advertisements on the back page. *Star* reporters always found the evidence to support a crusade."

Nor did the *Tely* blush at repaying its sponsors. One day after Bassett had bought the paper on John David Eaton's signature, pictures of eight new Eaton's executives decorated Page One, a prominence that must have astonished even these former shoe clerks.

But the *Star* topped the bigotry-cum-bias poll early in the decade when, fanatic about keeping Tory George Drew out of the provincial premiership with a story manufacturing an "alliance" between Drew and Montreal mayor Camillien Houde, the *Star* election-day main line read:

KEEP CANADA BRITISH
DESTROY DREW'S HOUDE
GOD SAVE THE KING

The king was sacrificed in the last edition for VOTE ST. LAURENT—not much of an improvement.

But, as Bassett (unauthorized) biographer Maggie Siggins says, the *Tely* was hardly better. On learning that *The Star Weekly* didn't pay an 8 percent sales tax on newsprint, the *Tely* screamed LIBERALS PAYING OFF THE STAR.

These heads could not, of course, compare in reader interest with later ones in the *Tely*. Samples: RADIOACTIVE HUMAN ROAMS TORONTO STREETS; MAD DOG PERVERTS LOOSE—PRIEST BLAMES TV, BOOKS.

"We were," muses MacFarlane, "printing a tabloid in broadsheet form."

Part of the grist for the tabloid mill involved the worst job on any newspaper—the picture pickup. This ugly, miserable, soul-destroying business meant going to the house of a murder victim, the mother of a child killed in an accident or some such horror, and asking her for a photograph of the newly deceased. Sometimes we got there before the cops and would have to break the news. We always tried to get there before the *Star* and scoop up everything.

Picture pickups are an ancient tradition. Ben Hecht, in his book about newspapering in New York in the twenties, tells of climbing up on the roof of a house where the widow of a gangland victim lived and covering the smoking chimney with a piece of wood. The smoke forced the grieving widow out and Hecht ran inside and grabbed a picture off the piano.

We had to lie, cry, sometimes get down on our knees and pray with the family in return for a blurred photograph. To get the entire photograph album was the ultimate triumph. On one occasion, I had to tell the mother of a young girl, stabbed by her boyfriend in a schoolyard, that we had a revealing picture of her daughter taken at the beach that we would have to use unless she gave us another. She did. I felt rotten. So you go and get drunk.

Once in a while, when the other paper had a picture you couldn't get, you copied it. Harry Hindmarsh, a member of the ruling family and an editor in the razzmatazz days, says the *Star* had developed a photographic technique for copying *Tely* pictures so the screen of dots, common to all zinc plates then, did not show.

"It drove the *Tely* mad," says Hindmarsh. "We could always be sure to have their pix by the next edition."

Once, in a plane crash in Amos, Quebec, the *Tely* had an exclusive six-column picture of the wreckage. The *Star* copied it and played it even bigger. MacFarlane called the *Star*, swearing vengeance, but he knew it was hopeless. Hindmarsh just laughed.

Whatever happened, the grisly pix had to be picked up or copied. And, if worse came to worst, and the victim wasn't too badly damaged, I'd go down to the morgue, prop the corpse's eyelids open with bits of toothpick, and there he was in the paper, as lively as ever.

All this lying, the stomach-turning gore of accidents, the cheap cynicism in the face of tragedy, the awful smell of burned flesh at fires, the stink of police cells and the day-to-day horrors of tabloid journalism forms a shell after a while. You stop feeling. Like cops maybe. And it's fatal to good storytelling. So you try to keep caring, keep feeling wretched or triumphant or whatever. But it's hard, especially on wives. Getting home at night after a day of blood and smoke and someone else's agony, to be asked to share the dismay—genuine enough—of the baby's near accident involved a gearing-down that many of us never did master.

Sometimes travellers would reach Toronto from other papers, bringing their own tales to match ours. A few wrote about them in a book called *Canadian Newspapers: The Inside Story.*

On some papers, the unhappy reporters have written, the editing was at best rudimentary. Harry Flemming of the Halifax *Chronicle-Herald*—which the Davey Committee accused of "lazy, uncaring journalism"—told book editor Walter Stewart of some malaprops. A *Herald* review wrote of "Duke Ellington's jazz classic 'Move Into Go.'" But Flemming's favorite was the *Herald* reporter who asked singer Buffy Sainte-Marie why she didn't wear Indian costume at her performances. "Because," the paper had her saying, "I don't want to look like a pocco hontis."

On *The Telegram*, meanwhile, Bassett was flying off in all directions—hiring columnists, firing editors, conducting grand royal tours of Europe with his wife and managing to make Page One interviewing the Great Ones from David Ben-Gurion to Anthony Eden.

One day he decided the *Tely* should go Sunday. It lasted four months and cost him. Doug MacFarlane was against it from the beginning because it broke the law, the Lord's Day Act. But for the nineteen editions it lasted, they all threw themselves into making it a success.

And there were some good stories. I got a call one day from a friend of mine in Kingston Penitentiary.

"You got a telephone in your cell?" I asked.

"Nope," he said. "The guy in the next block has tuberculosis. I had him spit in a test-tube and turned it in as mine. They moved me to the hospital wing. Great place, no locks. I'm in a restaurant across the street from the pen.

"Now, why I called," he said, "is this. There's a guy here, a murderer, who has been taking training as a medical orderly. The other day they let him out to visit a hospital in Kingston and he was in the operating room when one of Kingston's highfalutin ladies had her baby."

"My goodness," I said "I'll drive right down. Can't have murderers in operating rooms, even in Kingston."

The story turned out to be perfectly true, but the warden had a fit when I asked him about it. And an even bigger one, after the Sunday *Tely* played it on Page One, and I returned to Kingston Pen to thank my friend. "Great job," he yelled from his cell window. "You screwed the sonovabitch."

I had, as well, the warden pointed out, destroyed the man's rehabilitation program.

As the fifties wore on, the *Tely*'s circulation continued to climb. When Bassett bought the paper in 1952, its circulation was 210,177 and by 1957 it had risen to 268,343. But that turned out to be its peak while the *Star*'s kept climbing.

Bee Honderich has a number of explanations.

"One of the things that helped us was that the *Star* reflected a pretty liberal view, a concern for the underdog. The only way you could justify all the slaughter of the war was that you were going to create a better society. There was a liberal mood in the country and we were at the leading edge of the liberal trend.

"The people who put the *Tely* together (in the fifties) were very clever, very smart," Honderich says. "But I don't think they helped themselves when they made a great play for Jewish readers. [The *Tely* had a rabbi as an editorial writer and sent him to cover the Arab-Israeli wars.] That may have got them Jewish readers but it offended others. Now, that may have been a matter of principle but I don't think it looked that way."

Honderich also points out that not all newspaper battles are won in the editorial room. "I think what you print in the paper is the basic element, but the *Star* had great strengths in advertising and circulation. I don't think *The Telegram* had depth in those areas and that was the important thing."

Bassett knew what was happening: every paper the *Tely* printed lost money because the circulation couldn't justify higher ad rates while costs—newsprint, salaries, ink—were the same at the *Tely* as at the *Star*.

"We were between a rock and a hard place all the time," he says, "day after day, year after year."

But with Eaton's backing—and his indifference to losses—Bassett drove the paper on, having a wonderful time.

"Those were great, exciting days," says MacFarlane. "In my lifetime, there was never a period to match those whoop-de-do years. We didn't hurt anybody. We may have embellished. We may have stretched. But there was always a hard kernel of fact there."

There was certainly no doubt about the fact that on a September day in 1949 a man walked into the Bank of Montreal branch in Toronto's North York, waving a Luger pistol and demanding money. His name, it turned out later, was Eddie Boyd. The *Tely* and the *Star* gave it routine coverage.

But it was the beginning of a three-year criminal adventure, a cops-and-robbers story of sex, money and death, that started the two papers on a decade of razzle-dazzle rivalry. The Last Great Newspaper War had begun.

3 | Bullets, Blood and Breakouts

He had rouged his face and stuck cotton batting in his cheeks and his breath stank of whiskey. But what gave Edwin Alonzo Boyd a certain authority when he walked into the Armour Heights branch of the Bank of Montreal on a September morning in 1949 was a large, black Luger pistol.

He was a small man, thin-faced with a pencil moustache. He was very nervous and his hand shook as he pushed the note toward the teller: "Hold up—would you like to be a dead hero? Fill bag with money."

The teller began stuffing the canvas bag with cash and at the same time stepped on the alarm. "Hurry up," Eddie said, "there's going to be a lot of dead people around here if you don't."

Finally, the cash drawer was empty. Boyd grabbed the bag and ran out to the street where he tried to push his way into a parked car. Bullets thunked off the car trunk. The bank manager was firing at him. Eddie ran. He stumbled across a yard, spilling part of the loot. At the bus stop, the bus was just pulling away. The hell with it; he'd walk to his truck parked a few blocks away. After all, it was a nice day and later he would discover there was $2,200 in the canvas bag.

This was Eddie Boyd's first bank robbery. In later years when he headed the most infamous bank-robbing gang in Canadian history, he would learn to do it much more smoothly. The Toronto afternoon papers, the *Star* and *The Telegram*, would keep a casual eye on Eddie's exploits at first. After all, bank robbery wasn't exactly novel in Toronto. There had been the Polka Dot Gang and the Numbers Gang and, of course, Red Ryan, a notorious robber in the twenties who got religion in prison. He was paroled and then went out and killed a policeman during another bank stickup.

Eddie Boyd was not brand-new to crime. His father had been a Toronto cop and, when the Depression hit, Eddie left home to bum around the west. He'd spent six weeks in jail in Edmonton for vagrancy and in Calgary he'd ordered a meal of stewed beef, topped off with an ice-cream dish called a Rainbow Special, with no money to pay. In sentencing him to three days in the tank, the magistrate said: "I can understand you were hungry . . . but a Rainbow Special?" Eddie always had a bit of class.

In time he joined the army, served as a commando in Europe and married a pretty English dance teacher named Doreen Mary Frances Thompson. When he came back from the war, Eddie got a job driving a streetcar in Toronto. The Boyd Gang's historians, Marjorie Lamb and Barry Pearson, say that one day Eddie read in the papers about a retarded, sixteen-year-old kid who walked into a bank with a gun and walked out with $69,000. It seemed to Eddie—who had quit his job on the streetcars and was washing windows—that if some nut kid could do it, he could do it even better.

That's when he collected the Luger he'd brought back from the war and walked into the Bank of Montreal.

In the next couple of years, Edwin Boyd robbed three more banks, including another run at the Armour Heights branch. The teller couldn't believe her eyes. His wife, Doreen, confronted him one day, as he was washing the rouge off his face. "I just heard about the robbery on the radio."

"What about it?" said Eddie.

"It was you, wasn't it?"

"Yes," said Eddie.

Doreen was neither angry nor shocked. When he got a good job, she was sure, he would reform.

By now, however, the Toronto cops were getting irritated about the unprecedented number of bank robberies by Boyd and others around Toronto. Two outstanding detectives, Dolph Payne and The Chinaman, were especially annoyed. Dolph, a big, amiable redheaded man, was in on the first investigation that nailed Boyd for a bungled stickup at a Dominion Bank. The Chinaman, whose real name was Edmund Tong, would meet the gang in person later. And die.

The police reporters on the afternoon papers, Gwyn (Jocko) Thomas on the *Star* and Doug Creighton and Herb Biggs on the *Tely*, were beginning to take an interest in Boyd as a bank robber who could sell papers when he was caught and sent to the Don Jail to await a preliminary hearing. It was while Eddie was in the coop that Lennie Jackson made his appearance. Lennie and a bunch of guys in Hallowe'en masks began hitting banks in small towns north of Toronto. Lennie was easy to recognize, however, because he had a wooden foot, the result of an accident in a railway yard. When Lennie and the boys held up a bank in Toronto, The Chinaman took over their case.

Tong was a Welshman, actually, an ex-rugby-player who did some of his best detective work hanging around taverns like the Horseshoe or the Silver Rail or the Metropole Hotel, listening to the clientele. Tong was looking for Lennie Jackson, who used to work at the Horseshoe, for the Toronto hit. On a hot summer day in 1951, he spotted him limping down a lane. Lennie was carrying a brown paper bag, and while there was nothing suspicious in that, Tong thought he'd pull him in. When Lennie saw The Chinaman, he threw the bag through the window of a car and took off, but Tong followed and brought him down with a rugby tackle. There was $1,500 of the bank's money in the paper bag and Lennie was sent to The Don.

On visitors' day at the Don Jail, Lennie's girlfriend, Ann Roberts, showed up sometimes with a friend of theirs, Steve Suchan, a very good-looking guy, born in Czechoslovakia. Steve's parents had named him Valent because he was born on St. Valentine's day, but he didn't like the name much and had changed it.

Steve had studied the violin for years and played very well. In fact, about the only things Steve liked better than his violin were girls and guns. One day, just after the war, he traded his violin for a .455 Smith and Wesson revolver. In the spring of 1951, Steve was doorman at the King Edward Hotel in Toronto and a professional gangster who joined Lennie Jackson in the bank-robbing business. He missed the hit that sent Lennie to jail but took an active interest in helping his buddies to escape.

In the cell block was another Jackson, Willie the Clown, who had been in and out of jail since he was sixteen. He was in this time for robbing an old man and beating him nearly to death with a beer bottle. He was, none the less, a funny, care-free fellow, always making faces and telling jokes.

So, on this day, October 25, 1951, there they were: The Boyd Gang. Three were on the inside, one on the outside. All of them plotting escape.

Near the end of their book on the gang, when there is blood on the street and The Chinaman lies dying, historians Lamb and Pearson muse briefly on the role of the *Star* and *Tely* in the whole business:

> The *Tely* served up some juicy tidbits that the *Star* failed to collect or did not choose to print. But on balance, the *Star* exploited the story more effectively than the *Telegram* and won this round in the battle for leadership that continued for another 20 years.
>
> The world of journalism was changing subtly. Readers were becoming more sophisticated and less willing to tolerate newspapers who sacrificed credibility to flamboyance. But in 1952 that sold newspapers and the two big Toronto dailies were locked in a circulation war. Crime stories broke fast and boosted circulation. Coverage had to be rapid and heavy. Journalists had little time to reflect that in the process of "getting the story" they were creating a myth. None of them realized the myth being created by the press was the phenomenon known as "The Boyd Gang."

While the two papers covered the bank holdups in the usual fashion, with sketches of the bank layouts, frightened tellers, brave managers and laconic cops, Eddie Boyd and the two Jacksons simply took over the front pages when they escaped from The Don.

The Don Jail was built in 1864. Tempered steel was scarce, then, so the bars were made of soft Russian iron. The sound of sawing was frequently heard as convicts ripped and twisted their way to freedom. In the first week of November, 1958, a cold time, Boyd was keeping warm by sawing away at the soft bars using a smuggled hacksaw. The cut was concealed with a mixture of soap and shoe polish. Sheets were collected from neighboring cells. When the bar finally gave, Eddie, Lennie and Willie squeezed through and slid down the sheets to the ground, inside the exercise yard. Other prisoners in the cell block answered the missing men's names at roll call so they weren't missed right away. The three men looped the twisted sheets over a projection in the eighteen-foot-high prison wall and, hand over hand, hauled themselves up and over. They ran to Suchan's apartment nearby.

In the *Tely* Norm Johnson told just about the whole story in his lead: "Two bank bandit suspects, one with an artificial foot, and a convicted armed robber escaped yesterday from the Don jail by sawing through an iron bar of a second-story corridor window, climbing 46 feet down knotted bedclothes to the exercise yard and scaling an 18-foot brick wall."

Johnson didn't have the whole front page to himself, however. There was one story about Canadian troops fighting out of a trap in Korea and another about a chicken that hitchhiked a ride in a truck.

Now the Boyd Gang was ready to go to work. Their first score was a Bank of Toronto branch where they scooped up $4,300. The *Tely* reported a "toothless mastermind" directed the robbery from the door, shouting commands. This was likely Boyd, who would take out his false teeth before a robbery to disguise his appearance. The cops picked up Willie and Eddie and stuck them in a lineup. But the teller, Mrs. Joan Robinson, had trouble identifying them. "Did you see any pictures in the papers?" she was asked. "I don't remember." "What paper do you read?" "The *Daily Star*." "Do you remember seeing any pictures in the *Daily Star*?" "I don't remember. I don't read much besides the comics."

When the gang hit the Leaside branch of the Royal Bank they were moving with smooth precision. And Lennie Jackson had discovered how effective a machine gun was in cooling folks down. Later, Lennie would acquire two Thompson sub-machine guns, probably in Buffalo, where most of the gang's armaments came from. It was a legendary weapon designed by General John Thompson, director of arsenals in the United States in World War One. It could fire 800 rounds of .45-caliber ammunition a minute, and weighed over twenty pounds. Its gangland reputation was earned in Prohibition firefights, but it was also widely used in World War Two. Lennie hardly ever had to fire the thing. Sometimes he just tapped slow tellers on the arm with it and they filled the canvas bags with remarkable speed. Boyd favored his Luger and Suchan the .445 Smith and Wesson, although on one Buffalo trip, Steve bought seven guns, ranging from a Baretta to an army Colt .45.

The Leaside robbery netted them $46,207.13, the largest payoff in banking history for Toronto and the suburbs. Eddie and Doreen and the family moved to Pickering and began building a house, while the rest of the gang shifted operations to Montreal.

A blues musical, *The Girls in the Gang*, based on the Boyd Gang exploits, tells in poignant fashion what it was like to be a "crime dame," the woman at the back of a newspaper photograph, in court, visiting her man in jail, having babies and raising a family with guns in the cupboard. Doreen Boyd was the most stable of the bunch, always ready to stand by her man, get the kids into private school and patch up bullet wounds. Suchan had two girlfriends: one had a baby by him; the other, Mary Mitchell, betrayed him.

Mary was a friend of Eddie Tong and would visit him frequently at police headquarters to exchange crime gossip. She told the gang she was spying for them. One day in the spring of 1952, Mary went to Lennie and Steve and opened the front of her blouse to show burn marks on her breasts. She said The Chinaman had tortured her for information. She didn't tell them she had given Tong and his partner, Roy Perry, the license number of a black Monarch sedan which the gang was using, owned by Suchan's other girlfriend. The police reporters on the *Star* and the *Tely* didn't believe Tong would burn a woman with a cigarette—it just wasn't like him. Perhaps Mary burned herself, but she never admitted it.

On the morning of March 6, 1952, the Boyd Gang's reputation as a bunch of swashbuckling, but non-lethal, villains came to a bloody end.

Steve Suchan and Lennie Jackson were in the black Monarch heading north out of mid-town Toronto when Edmund Tong and Roy Perry in police cruiser D-5 spotted them. The Chinaman didn't know Suchan but he knew Lennie. The cruiser ran alongside the Monarch, Tong rolled down the window and yelled, "Pull over to the curb, boys."

What happened next, Perry told the *Tely* later, was "thirty seconds of hell".

Lamb and Pearson describe it:

> Suchan was terrified. He had a wanted man in his car and had harboured Boyd, the RCMP's tenth most wanted criminal, to say nothing of his own criminal activities. There would be a scandal. His family would be involved. Blind panic seized him. He picked up his .455 Smith and Wesson and fired through the open window.
>
> The slug tore through the soft flesh of Tong's left breast, ripping through his lung. Its path was almost horizontal, and the tissue barely slowed it down. Passing through the spinal cavity, the bullet severed the spinal cord, finally coming to rest under Tong's right shoulder blade.

Tong went down. Lennie grabbed his gun and began firing at the police car's engine. Roy Perry threw himself onto the seat but he had been hit in the arm. He passed out.

Suchan gunned the black Monarch and sped away.

The papers were on the scene in minutes, flashing their cameras as Tong was lifted into an ambulance. The *Tely*'s Herb Biggs followed Tong and Chief of Detectives John Nimmo right into the hospital room. He wrote:

> He watched for a moment as the big, athletic chest of Edmund Tong rose and fell under the blanket. Insp. Nimmo watched as his best friend fought for his life. Then he bent closer to Tong's head and murmured a question. "Eddie", he asked, "who did this to you?" At first there was no answer. Gently Insp. Nimmo raised his friend's head from the pillow. He held a handful of pictures in front of the man's eyes. Recognition gleamed as the wounded man recognized one of the rogues gallery shots. "That's him", he whispered. It was a photograph of Steve Suchan.

The *Star* carried pictures of Boyd, Suchan and Jackson with the headline: HUNTED. The *Tely*'s Dorothy Howarth reported that Mrs. Tong "bore the tragedy with all the courage of her Highland Scot nature. A policeman's wife has got to expect this, she said." Later, when Ev Tong went to visit her husband in hospital, Eddie asked her how she was getting along. He was worried about her being alone.

"I was all right," she said. "I had a girlfriend with me."

"Oh, did you? Who was she?"

"Alex Gibb of the *Star*," answered Mrs. Tong.

Eddie and Doreen Boyd, who were at the movies, saw the headlines when they came out. They were stunned. They bought enough groceries to last a week, went home and locked themselves in.

Suchan and Jackson, meanwhile, in an absolute frenzy, were racing about the western part of Toronto in taxis until they finally headed for Montreal. In his apartment there, Suchan strapped on three handguns and loaded up with forty-seven rounds of ammunition. He figured to go down like

James Cagney. The police, in fact, already had him spotted from a telegraph receipt they'd found on his girlfriend in Toronto. When they broke into his room, guns firing, Suchan took three slugs, two in the chest and one in his hand, before he could draw any of his heavy weapons.

"Why don't you give it to me in the head?" Suchan said to the cop who had hit him. "Why don't you finish me?" He was hauled off to hospital and manacled to the bed instead. *The Telegram* said, "Steve Suchan had a big lobster dinner—as well as two loaded .45s under his belt—when he walked into a police ambush in his posh apartment last night."

The Montreal police had located Lennie Jackson as well. They went into his apartment, guns blazing, while Lennie screamed and fired back until his gun was empty. Then they tear-gassed him and he quit.

"Did I hit any cops?" he asked. No, he was told. "Geez, that's good. I was hoping I hadn't hurt any of them."

Meanwhile, in Toronto, the hunt was up for Eddie Boyd. Doug Creighton, the *Tely*'s police reporter, was sent to Hamilton on a tip he had been spotted there. Creighton thought that was nuts: Boyd had to be in Toronto, but he went anyway. No sooner had he arrived when he heard on his car radio that Boyd had been picked up at 42 Heath Street in Toronto. Creighton grabbed a reverse telephone directory and looked up the number of the Heath Street house and phoned. Dolph Payne answered.

"Dolph," Creighton said, "are there any *Tely* photographers there yet?"

"No," said Payne, "but the mayor's here."

"Oh Jesus, Dolph, don't move Boyd until the *Tely* gets there. Please."

Dolph agreed he might just hang on a while.

Payne had located Boyd in a masterly piece of police craft

that was meticulously detailed in the papers over the next few days. It involved a car that Doreen Boyd owned. Payne figured Doreen might want to sell it if they were on the run, so, day after day, he ran his finger down the classified ads in both papers. On March 10 his patience and instinct paid off. There it was in the *Tely*: "49 Austin, radio, heater, new tires and battery. $850."

Payne set up a baby-faced detective and a police stenographer as a couple looking for a car. They flushed Doreen and located Boyd. Payne burst through the door and leaped on Eddie Boyd, who was in bed.

"Well," said Boyd, when he'd untangled himself, "this is one way to meet you."

Boyd, obviously a *Tely* reader, had written a letter to the paper, which he never mailed. It was found in his room.

"Keep out of my way . . ." it warned, "start guarding your families . . . for I am no longer a respecter of persons. Death has always been a friend to me and I will meet it face to face. So keep out of my way and avoid bloodshed. Death means nothing to me when I am fighting for my family."

Mayor Allan Lamport—Lampy—was told of Boyd's impending capture and arrived on the scene, unshaved and without breakfast, to get in on the fun. He was photographed with Payne and others huddled over the briefcase where Boyd kept his cash and guns.

The *Tely* said "a faint smile flitted across Boyd's thin lips when he was led out of the house by police. Posing obligingly for photographers (the *Tely* men had got there at last) he turned to Mayor Lamport and asked: 'Should I smile?'

"The mayor was grim as he snapped: 'I wouldn't if I was in your position.'"

Tong managed a faint smile when he was told of Boyd's capture.

Then, on March 23, 1952, the Toronto police issued a bulletin: "Attention all divisions. Information received from Dr. Tovee at 12:30 A.M. this date that Sgt. of Dets. Ed Tong has just passed away at the Toronto General Hospital."

Now it was murder.

In the Don Jail, an unbelievable thing was happening—the Boyd Gang was herded together in the same cell block. Eddie Boyd, no longer the gentleman bandit, was tired and defeated. The warden had installed a microphone in the ceiling of his cell. He thought about suicide.

Willie the Clown had been picked up in Montreal a year earlier. He'd wandered into the washroom in a nightclub, opened his suitcoat and startled the gentleman at the next urinal by revealing a .45 revolver stuck in his belt. The cops arrived shortly and Willie got two years in Kingston Penitentiary. But Boyd hardly had been led into his Don Jail cell before Willie arrived. He had been transferred to The Don to face new charges arising from his bank-robbing career. Boyd was delighted to have someone familiar to talk to, and Willie was always good for a laugh. They were in adjoining cells.

Lamb and Pearson, who had the extraordinary good luck to interview Boyd years later, when he was on parole and living out west, compiled a detailed picture of Boyd's life in The Don in this period. It was a curious time.

Boyd was practising mental tricks, mind-reading and the like. Sometimes he prayed, but to Satan instead of God. And he talked to Willie about getting out. Willie figured it would be pretty tough. They were on death row.

Then, one day, to the surprise and delight of Willie and Eddie, Lennie Jackson arrived. He was in a cast and they had taken his artificial foot away, but he was back with his buddies.

Finally, to complete the cast, Steve Suchan showed up, pus

draining from a tube in his side. Now the four cells in death row were full. The Boyd Gang was together again. "It was almost as if the cops were challenging them to do something," Doreen Boyd said later. "Escape again or something."

At first they were all locked in their cells. But, after a while, the warden relented and they were allowed out in the corridor together to play chess and talk. About this time, Boyd later told the gang's biographers, he began to lose interest in escaping, but he felt obliged to give the others a hand.

First, they needed a hacksaw. A man arrived to visit Willie one day and, out of the blue, offered to help them to escape. He has not been identified publicly, but was a respectable businessman who later—to the great satisfaction of the police—went broke. The Boyd Gang's breakout would have been impossible without him. They asked him to bring them in a key blank and a file. He couldn't get the blank but showed up with a shoehorn and a file. Boyd would later tell *Telegram* reporter Norman Johnson that a key was made from a spoon and a tin-cup handle.

One of the guards was a friendly, ex-policeman who liked to kibitz with Willie. Willie grabbed the guard's key one day as he was locking Suchan in his cell and pressed it firmly into his palm. Laughing, he gave the key back but the impression remained. Willie grabbed a pencil and transferred the pattern from his palm onto his cell wall. He was now ready to file a key. The boys would yowl "Down by the old mill stream . . ." under the ceiling microphone while Boyd filed away. When it was done, he tried it on Suchan's cell door and, after a little adjustment, it worked perfectly. They were now ready for the businessman to supply a hacksaw. They promised him $7,000 from their first, post-escape bank job and he showed up with the saw.

Each morning just before daybreak, Boyd would unlock the cell door and get busy on the bars while the others held pillows over the ceiling microphone. The tried-and-true mixture of soap and shoe polish covered the cuts. Finally, they were ready. They would squeeze through the bars, walk along the top of the wall and jump down outside. Boyd went first—and got stuck. Willie tried, with butter smeared on his naked hips. The damn opening was too small. They'd have to cut a second bar. This time they put a nail through each end of the hacksaw blade and taped them for handles. Then Willie and Eddie could saw back and forth. On September 8, 1952 they were ready. It was their last chance because the next day Suchan and Jackson were scheduled to go on trial for murder.

Boyd went first, out along the wall, followed by the others. They lay down while a guard below finished his shift and left. Then, one by one, they dropped down and began running up the Don Valley.

They'd done it. The Boyd Gang had escaped from the Don Jail, not once, but twice.

There were killers and robbers on the loose and the papers went wild.

BOYD, KILLER PALS ON LOOSE

POLICE "SHOOT ON SIGHT"

HUSBAND WON'T BE TAKEN ALIVE—MRS. BOYD

screamed the *Tely*.

REWARD $4,000 FOR EACH

BOYD, SUCHAN, 2 JACKSONS

SAW WAY OUT OF JAIL

said the *Star*.

At the *Tely*, Doug MacFarlane ordered everyone out of the city room. "Get the hell out and find Boyd," he said. I wasn't too enthusiastic about confronting a gang of killers for the greater joy of *The Telegram*, but what the hell, it was a great story, so I went. So did dozens of other reporters. Our cars sped along the back roads north of The Don, stopping only to peer into barns, hoping the Boyds weren't inside.

The *Star's* Buck Johnston remembers it was a "wild afternoon": "We scoured the then-empty reaches of Scarborough for the escapees. Sums of money were offered local farmers for information leading to their whereabouts. At times, *Star* vehicles were chasing *Tely* cars and vice versa in the mistaken belief that the Boyd gang had been apprehended."

North of Scarborough the searchers found themselves among the country estates of Toronto's millionaires. With cars speeding up to barns, disgorging reporters and racing away again, there hadn't been so much excitement since the last fox hunt.

Best of all, people were buying papers as fast as we could get them out on the streets.

Gordon Sinclair of the *Star*, in a copyrighted story, announced, "The Edwin Boyd gang had active plans . . . and may still have these plans . . . to stick up two, three or even four banks at the same time in the Toronto district. They told me this themselves." Somewhat indirectly as it turned out. Sinclair said he had been approached by Doreen Boyd—"an attractive soft-voiced woman with penetrating, almost hypnotic eyes"— to write the Boyd Gang's story and had offered some teasing revelations. They were to split the fee. Sinclair turned her down.

Lampy said the escape was "Toronto's greatest shame."

The *Tely* had a reporter photographed squeezing through a hole in a cardboard box exactly the same dimensions—9¼" by 13¼"—as the cell window with the sawed bars. Dorothy Howarth, in an exclusive interview with Doreen Boyd, learned that Mrs. Boyd "has only one loyalty and this to her husband. 'If it had been murder or rape,' she said, 'I might feel differently. But Ed never hurt anyone. Only the banks and they're heavily insured. They don't lose anything.'"

The next day, the *Tely* "opened its columns as a public service" for Mrs. Boyd to write a letter advising Eddie to give himself up. Lampy said, in the *Tely*, that *The Telegram* was "rendering a public service" in printing the letter adding: "The hunt is on and the police are never going to give up. They have instructions to shoot to kill."

Mrs. Boyd also decided to get her appeal on the radio. "The kids and I have been through a lot this last year," she told the *Tely*. "Now it has all started again, only much worse. I want Ed to realize our lot, the kids and mine, is much tougher than his. He suffers a physical prison, we suffer a mental prison."

The younger Boyd children, eight-year-old twin boys, the *Tely* reported, "can't figure out what's happening. All they know is that their Mommy is awfully upset at what their Dad is doing and whatever it is they wish he wouldn't."

"Remember, Eddie," Mrs. Boyd pleaded on the airwaves, "from our point of view peace of mind means an awful lot."

Eddie, out in the woods, didn't have a radio.

Premier Leslie Frost ordered an inquiry and fired eight Don jailers.

The *Star* reported that a girl in Hawkesbury near the Quebec border had sold Boyd some peroxide and makeup. Four men were seen changing clothes near Brampton. A U.S. penal expert allowed as how supervision was best when it came to keeping men in the coop. Jocko Thomas reported that officials thought the hole in the window was too small to crawl through and the Boyd Gang had probably walked out the back door of the Don Jail. The *Tely* said that, on the first newspaper tour of the death cells, they discovered that Eddie

Boyd was taking Bible lessons but he'd left the Scriptures behind.

Lampy continued working up a head of steam. At a plowing match with Ottawa's mayor Charlotte Whitton, he allowed: "What fool put those four in the same cell block with club-car privileges? The place was so wide open they could have walked out the front door. All they wanted was a cocktail bar."

Because Boyd was supposed to be a master of disguise, the *Star* figured the whole gang might be disguised. So the paper published a series of pictures showing Suchan dressed as a female nurse, a male bus driver and a female transit guide. They had Eddie Boyd as a laborer, a chauffeur and a fireman.

Meanwhile, up the Don Valley, the Boyd Gang was hustling along. Lennie Jackson had a tin cup stuck on the stump of his leg. Willie Jackson was sent to scrounge food and returned with bread, cheese and sausage. They slept under trees and kept heading north, hoping to find an abandoned farm where they could hole up.

Their businessman friend had arranged for a cache of guns and food to be hidden at a dump on Sheppard Avenue, several miles away. Meantime, a helicopter whirred overhead. They'd have to keep low. Nearly a week had gone by and they were still in the valley and on the loose.

Out near Whitby, a chicken farmer heard a suspicious noise near the henhouse, so he grabbed his gun, raised the window and saw a man limping along. "As soon as I saw him limping, I thought it was Lennie Jackson," he said. "So I fired." The .22 bullet got a patient at the Ontario Psychiatric Hospital in the seat of the pants.

Then a Scarborough cop spotted a suspicious-looking black car with a beat-up license plate. He chased it at speeds up to 75 mph, firing warning shots. It must be the Boyds, he figured, especially when passengers in the car began firing back. Two bullets missed him by inches. He swerved and hit a tree. The car got away. It wasn't the Boyd Gang.

The Malvern area swarmed with police and reporters but when the gang finally came out of the woods and headed for a barn, no one spotted them. It looked like a good place, except Lennie Jackson was sniffling and wheezing from all the hay and dust.

At *The Globe and Mail*, a reporter called Grey Hamilton, was told he had a phone call. It was a friend, Bert Powell, manager of the Canadian National Exhibition. Powell owned a farm north of Toronto and he thought Grey ought to know there were some men in a nearby barn and he had called the police. Hamilton grabbed a photographer and headed up Don Mills Road. He got to the barn, just as two North York detectives, Maurice Richardson and Bert Trotter, opened the door with their guns drawn. Inside was the Boyd Gang, caught without weapons and prepared to surrender.

Hamilton had a clean beat and the usually staid *Globe* exploded with a head in end-of-the-world type: NAB BOYD GANG.

The outlaws were taken to the North York Police station, which quickly became a carnival. Lampy was there in minutes, of course. Photographers and reporters swarmed around the cells. Willie Jackson and Eddie Boyd laughed and joked, posing for pictures. Willie called Lampy over to his cell. I joined the mayor. "You want to know how we escaped?" Willie asked the mayor. "Come closer and I'll whisper it." We both leaned toward the cell bars. "I hypnotized the guards," Willie bellowed. Lampy reared back, furious.

"Mr. Mayor," said Suchan, "I hope we proved something about the Don Jail."

Eddie Boyd said he'd saw his way out of The Don again in a month. "You'd better not," said Detective Inspector Archie

McCathie. "I haven't been in bed before three A.M. since you got out." "That won't hurt you, you're too fat anyway," said Eddie Boyd, laughing.

The *Tely*, boasting of an exclusive by Norm Johnson, had Boyd tell his own story: "I took off 20 pounds to squeeze through that little hole we cut in the bars and then I put in the worst nine days of my life."

The gang was sent back to the Don Jail, to the same four cells from which they had escaped. But this time they had armed guards for company, twenty-four hours a day. Within a week they would go on trial: Steve Suchan and Leonard Jackson for murder; Eddie Boyd on eleven charges of bank robbery; Willie Jackson for, among other things, escaping custody.

Suchan and Jackson obviously needed the best criminal lawyers they could find. And they got them—Arthur Maloney agreed to defend Jackson at the request of Chief Justice McRuer. In his office, John J. Robinette was approached by his cleaning woman who said her son was in trouble and would Mr. Robinette defend him. He went to the Don Jail to talk to Steve Suchan.

J.J. Robinette was among a half-dozen top criminal lawyers in Toronto. Some said he was the best. An elegant, sensitive man, he seldom raised his voice in court. And he seldom lost a major case. Arthur Maloney, then in his ninth year of practise, would blossom into a brilliant defense counsel. Jack Batten, in his book *In Court*, described Maloney as "sweet-talking and loquacious, as Irish as a glass of Bushmill's Whiskey (a drink he wouldn't turn away). He's a fervent Catholic and his sense of religion, a mix of hard-line righteousness and genial kindliness, suggests he may have made a swell priest, part thundering Jesuit, part Bing Crosby in *Going My Way*."

Robinette told Batten he found Suchan "a kindly sort of

fellow. At the trial, when it was his life that was at stake, he worried more about the way I was taking it than he did about himself. His basic trouble was laziness. He got in with these other fellows, holdup men, and he thought, gee, this is an easy way to make money."

The best the pair of lawyers could hope for was manslaughter. After all, Tong was dead. Suchan's defense would be that he fired at the car engine to disable it and Jackson hadn't shot at all. But one of the damning pieces of evidence—provocative to the jury—was a dressmaker's dummy found in the house where Suchan and Jackson had been hiding. It had bullet holes in the heart.

Doreen Boyd was in court every day, wearing a scarlet coat that became her trademark. The *Tely* noted she was "hatless" in a place, like a church, where women were supposed to wear hats.

Maloney's defense of Jackson wasn't going well. Jackson was impatient and belligerent. He refused to be led by Maloney. He virtually admitted he knew Suchan had a gun and that he was prepared to use it. "I was shattered," Maloney recalled later. "I knew he'd thrown in the sponge. I asked him later, why. 'If those bastards, that prosecutor, that judge, want me that bad, hell, I'm going to give myself to them.'"

Then Jackson said to his lawyer: "I let you down, didn't I?" "You didn't let me down," said Maloney, "you let yourself down."

Finally, it was over. The jury came back with their verdict for both men: guilty as charged.

Chief Justice McRuer, his voice soft and trembling, then pronounced sentence on both men, the most awful words in the English language: "You shall be taken to the place from whence you came and there kept in close detention until the 16th of December, 1952, and thence you shall be taken to the place of execution, and there be hanged by the neck until you are dead. May God have mercy on your soul."

Robinette turned to Maloney at the defense table. "My God," he said, "I've never heard those words before."

Suchan and Jackson looked straight ahead, their faces impassive.

As they were led out of court, Lamb and Pearson report, Suchan mumbled to Jackson "And they call that justice."

Lennie, gently chiding, replied: "Of course that's justice. We killed a man didn't we?"

Edwin Alonzo Boyd drew a life sentence. Willie Jackson got twenty years. "Boyd's sunken cheeks twitched when he heard the sentence," the *Tely* reported. "He hugged his wife, who whispered a few words, and then they were torn apart."

Dorothy Howarth of the *Tely* noted the Community Chest girls' choir sang "My Own Dear Land" on the front steps of the courthouse as the outlaws were led out the back. "I have a life sentence to serve, too," Doreen Boyd told Howarth. "When they sentenced Ed, they sentenced me." The *Tely*'s Allan Kent offered a little sermon on the front page of the paper, just below a picture of a smiling Boyd and Jackson, cigar jutting from his mouth, being led from court.

"The law proved itself today a bigger, more potent force in the Canadian community than any evil confederacy of law-breakers no matter how shrewd, how bold, how well organized. The judge and jury have dealt the coup-de-grace to the notorious Boyd gang, one of the most ruthless bands of criminals and law flouters ever to challenge society's supreme authority in this country."

Suchan and Jackson were now alone on Death Row; Boyd and Willie Jackson had been sent to Kingston Penitentiary.

The charges against Doreen Boyd of harboring a fugitive were dismissed and police were forced to give back her belongings. Among them was a box of Tampax. It was very valuable because, a while back, when Eddie was flush, he'd pulled the cotton out of the cylinders and stuffed them with $100 bills. There was $6,000 in the box.

On Death Row, Suchan and Jackson found religion. Batten said it was Maloney's doing. Suchan's mother, the cleaning woman, had approached him as a co-religionist, regretful that her son had left the church and asking if Maloney could coax him back.

"Maloney recruited Father John Kelly, a Catholic priest who later became president of St. Michael's College in Toronto and, in daily visits to Suchan, Kelly brought him around to his old Catholicism," Batten wrote.

Jackson, although Jewish, followed and asked to be baptized in the Catholic faith. He took to his new religion with such enthusiasm that he asked that his final meal before his execution be the same as that offered at the Last Supper. But he had to settle for more routine fare—fried chicken, apple pie, ice cream and a cigar.

Suchan read Robinette a letter he had written to his mother: "I know I'll join my brothers who have gone before me now, but I'm not afraid at all, and you, Momma, be strong and don't cry for me. I beg you.

"Straight from my heart I love you Momma. And my small brother, a million times. Please forgive me, Momma, for bringing you so much sorrow. By bye, mother Dear. Your son, Valent. XXXXXX"

The pair were to be hanged just after midnight. Reporters gathered outside the Don Jail walls, freezing in the December air. There was a crowd of the curious as well. The *Tely*'s Dick O'Hagan was assigned to spend the final hours with Mrs. Suchan at her home. He did not relish the job.

Reporter George Brimmell was told to collect any last words from the two men.

As midnight approached, the pair were injected with a sedative. They became calm, almost cheerful. Lennie asked for his wooden foot back for the walk to the gallows, but his request was refused.

Suchan, Brimmell reported, was led from the death cell first. He was pale. The room was freezing. He had neither shoes nor shirt. "No one ever told me we'd be freezing to death," Suchan said. "I thought we were hanging. Hurry up, Lennie. I don't want to freeze to death."

As the pair stepped on the steel trapdoor, nooses around their necks, Suchan turned to Father Kelly. "Don't worry, Father, it won't hurt." Black hoods were dropped over their heads, and hangman Jack Ellis pulled the lever. Forty-five minutes later they were pronounced dead.

A few days later, Mrs. Suchan, impressed by Dick O'Hagan's story of the death-watch at her home, sent him a pair of warm, woollen socks.

Her son no longer had any use for them.

4 | Fabian of the Yard

The girl had no time to scream. A soaked chloroform pad was pressed upon her face. Arms pinioned her viciously. Her first gasp had sucked the acrid narcotic fumes into her throat, and as the liquid burned her lips she gurgled with helpless fear. Then dizziness roared over her like rushing water . . . her body dropped limply upon the pavement.

The attacker stirred her unceremoniously with his polished shoe, picked up her handbag, wrenched a trivial nine-carat ring from her finger, and hastened softly away. A few dazed moments afterwards she staggered to her feet, her eyes still streaming from the pungent ether, her fair hair disordered, her clothes rumpled and smirched from road dirt.

She was brought to the Divisional Inspector's Office at the station. "It's our chum with the ether again, sir," said the fatherly police sergeant as he helped her into a chair. [Fabian] sighed . . . .

Ian Paterson put the book down on the rewrite desk and said to no one in particular, "I bet Fabian could find Marion McDowell."

Rewrite chief George Brimmell glanced at the title of the book, *Fabian of the Yard.* "You mean the Scotland Yard guy? Well, maybe . . . . Why don't you see if we can get him over here?"

It was August, 1953, the doldrums of summer, and Paterson was anxious to stir up something. He hadn't had a decent story in *The Telegram* for weeks. Besides he liked excitement. Since he had left England for a job on the *Tely* a couple of years ago things had been too damn quiet. Although he'd stayed out of trouble. Not like back home.

Paterson was a young Scot who was born to make trouble. In the army, he had fallen into so many fine messes in southeast Asia that his various commanders had finally dispatched him to the lowest job in the remotest corner of the Empire—tending mules in the Khyber Pass.

But it wasn't low enough or far enough. One day, leading his mules laden with ammunition along a high trail above the pass, Paterson got the lead mule tangled up and the whole pack of squealing animals went over the side. The series of explosions that followed had every British soldier within miles out of his tent and staring wildly at the smoking hillside.

Back in England, Paterson got a job with Metro-Goldwyn-Mayer as publicist. His first task was to promote a new film, to be premiered in Edinburgh, called *Captain Horatio Hornblower RN.* It starred Gregory Peck as a naval commander in the Napoleonic wars. Paterson had a local fellow construct a papier-mâché replica of the prow of Hornblower's ship on the theater marquee. On opening night, he was to fire a small charge from a cannon when the celebrities arrived.

Everything went swimmingly. The sidewalk in front of the theater was filled with beautiful people, crowds swarmed, searchlights criss-crossed the sky, Paterson beamed, the cannon went off . . . and the whole prow collapsed in a giant mess of paper, rope and sail onto the screaming people below.

Paterson was fired.

Next, he went to work for the Billy Butlin Camps people, promoting the seashore joys of a Butlin holiday. The first day, visiting a camp, he learned a lifeguard had saved a child from drowning. Paterson got the name and home town of every child in the camp and wrote a story about the heroic rescue, inserting the name of a different child and different home town in each release. He sent them all to the local papers. It was not long before a British wire service, collecting stories from each town, concluded the children at this particular Billy Butlin camp were heading into the sea like lemmings.

Paterson was fired.

So he came to Canada and, not unnaturally, found a job on the craziest newspaper.

What Paterson was brooding about now was a case that had excited the *Tely* and the *Star* since the previous winter. It was the kidnapping of an attractive, seventeen-year-old girl from a car in a suburban lovers' lane, where she and her boyfriend had parked for an hour or so of this and that.

Her name was Marion Joan McDowell and she was a typist for an engraving firm. She lived in Scarborough, now part of Metro Toronto, with her very respectable parents. Scarborough was my beat for the *Tely* at the time, so I was involved from the beginning—which happened to be the night of December 6, 1958.

My first story, with only a few of the stops pulled out, led with: "A road-by-road, bush-by-bush search of Scarboro township was underway today for beautiful, 17-year-old Marion Joan McDowell, torn from her boyfriend's arms last night by a 'Lovers' Lane' bandit." There were plenty of stops to come.

Two years before, both papers had become equally exercised over the mysterious disappearance of another beautiful—all girls who made the papers in the fifties were beautiful—nineteen-year-old girl from York Township called Mabel Crumback.

Shortly after she did her flit, the *Tely*'s ace reporter, James Y. Nicol, left few stops in as he told readers: "Missing 13 days, Mabel Crumback, attractive [some girls were simply attractive], 19-year-old bookkeeper, today is the prisoner of a six-foot man with a harelip, if information given to provincial police is true. They are roaming Western Ontario in a car, the girl drugged and almost helpless. She is pleading 'O God, I hope no one else ever has to go through what has happened to me.'" Way down in the story, Nicol concedes that Mabel's mother doubted it was Mabel.

But a day or two later, *Tely* reporter Phil Murphy was soaring into pure poetry: "Fleet as a deer, wide-eyed in fear, in a bramble-torn blouse and shoes with high heels, a girl is hiding today somewhere in the lush farmland of Brant County." Mabel's mother was dubious about whether that curious creature was her daughter either.

But the rhythms of such tales had been clearly established, and Marion was well launched.

What we had to sell papers with this time was a classic crime story. I told it many, many times over the next few weeks.

One version I did went like this:

At 7 P.M. on the unusually warm summer night of Dec. 6, in an upstairs bedroom of [her] parents' home at 207 Oak Park Ave. in East York, Marion McDowell was dressing for a date. In front of her, ringing the vanity mirror of her dressing room table, were pictures of stage and screen stars. Many of them were autographed for Marion, an avid autograph collector. Behind her, over the bed was a crucifix. On a nearby wall was a calendar picturing a scantily-clad girl.

[In the fifties all attractive, beautiful girls wearing anything less than two pinafores and a fur coat were scantily clad.]

Marion was preparing for a date with Jimmy Wilson, a 19-year-old rigger for a scaffolding firm, with whom she had been out at least twice before. The girl, who stood five feet, three inches in her bare feet, with dark blonde hair, a round face and blue eyes, chose her clothes carefully. She put on a white blouse with black trimming and black buttons, a black wool skirt, a blue brushed nylon sweater coat and black, low-heeled shoes, laced high on the ankles. On her finger she wore a ring, a gift from her parents, initialled 'MM'.

Shortly after 7:30 P.M. she heard Jimmy Wilson blow the horn of his second-hand car, parked across the street outside. She went downstairs, said goodbye to her parents, Mr. and Mrs. Ross McDowell, promised not to be late, and went out the front door.

Her parents never saw her again.

Before picking her up Wilson had left his Kennedy Rd. home and driven to the Dainty Cafe on Danforth Ave., where he could be sure of meeting some of his teen-age friends. He spent a few minutes there, drinking a Coke. He left for Marion's house without telling his friends where he was going.

With Marion in the car, Wilson drove to an isolated part of Danforth Rd., a local Lovers' Lane. There was no car within 100 feet of where they parked, although they could make out the shapes of other cars parked farther away. For more than a half hour Marion and Jimmy sat in the front seat of the car and necked. They listened to the radio and smoked cigarettes.

Suddenly the door on Wilson's side of the car was wrenched open and a voice ordered Wilson out. He got

out. Wilson believed the man was wearing a knitted bala-
clava helmet and carrying a gun. He ordered Wilson to turn
around. He hit him once with what Wilson believed was
the butt of a gun. He hit him again as he was falling.

When Wilson came to he said he was in the back seat of
his own car with Marion, apparently unconscious, on top of
him. They were driven north on Danforth Rd. to an abandoned farm. The driver got out and lifted Marion from the
car. He carried her to another car parked ahead. Wilson
believed he saw him stuff the girl in the trunk.

Wilson scrambled over the front seat, found the key still
in the ignition and started the car. He backed out of the
farmyard, hitting a fence post once. Wilson drove up Danforth Rd., circled on a concession road and headed for
home. When he got home he told his parents what had
happened. After attending to his wound his parents drove
to the Scarboro police station.

Inspector of Detectives Harold Adamson listened to the
boy's tale and ordered an investigation. The hunt was on.

The *Star* quickly managed to establish two other necessary
characteristics of fifties girls. "She was a good girl and very
popular," they quoted her father. But the *Star* made a fatal mistake that would haunt them for weeks. They hustled the
McDowell family too hard while I oiled my way across the
kitchen floor. The McDowells would then not speak to the
beastly paper while they tolerated me.

The *Star*'s Buck Johnston recalls, "In the McDowell caper,
the *Tely* held all the cards, particularly access to the family.
After almost frantic orders from [city editor] Borden Spears, I
did manage to get into the McDowell house in the disguise of
a missionary student and offered a written prayer and a plea
for her release for the parents to sign."

The *Star* quickly located an astrologer—an essential figure in any missing-person story—for the paper. A. Fred Jackson of the Jackson Psychic School Inc. of Toronto was able to establish, a front-page story said, that Marion's slayer was "a former false friend of short stature, with broad shoulders, sharp, thin features, nose slightly hooked with small, restless eyes, dark brown or black hair and dull complexion."

It was a clean beat. But despite the detailed description, police were unable to locate the evil Scorpio.

Meanwhile, the *Tely* was cranking up fast. We had a strip of pictures illustrating a reenactment of the crime; our own, handwritten "heart-stirring appeal from her parents for some word of the whereabouts of their daughter"; and endless pictures of sober detectives pointing accusingly at the ground. I had also discovered the cops had found Marion's diary—"a little red book. The diary contains the names and addresses of all the beautiful blonde girl's boyfriends. Each name is being systematically checked, police said.

"'We will definitely be making an arrest in a day or two,' Scarboro Police Chief Wilf McLellan predicted this afternoon."

I was also able to report that the diary contained the names of bikers, whom Marion had been "riding pillion with."

Meanwhile, hundreds of high-school students were taking the afternoon off and swarming over Scarborough's barren fields.

In the early fifties, Scarborough was in the middle of a postwar land boom that would transform it into a residential-industrial complex of staggering banality. It would be called "Scarberia." But in 1954, there were vast stretches of empty fields, acres of bush, quarries and ponds. As more and more farmers were selling out to land developers, there were also a good many decaying farmhouses and barns. My family, my wife and two young children, lived in one old farmhouse, probably the last to survive in the central business area. We drew water from a well, had a barn stuffed, for some reason, with ancient CPR hotel furniture, and a disturbing neighbor.

He was a former German army machine-gunner and, when he got drunk, he would come over and explain to the wide-eyed children, with gestures: "Americans are stupid. They bunch up. You can get them all at once, rat-tat-tat. They would all go down in front of my gun. Stupid to bunch up. Don't do it kids." I don't think my children ever have.

The teenage searchers, later joined by the army, were everywhere, but all they managed to find were a couple of drunks in a barn who were sleeping so soundly the kids thought they were dead. Finally the pair woke up, had a refreshing couple of belts of shaving lotion and left.

Five days after Marion's kidnapping things were beginning to quiet down, newswise, until police chief McLellan came up with a pair of panties, a single shoe and a new theory.

Marion, he said, was alive and "had left Scarborough Township of her own free will."

Presumably knickerless and wearing only one shoe.

The panties—always described by both papers as "an undergarment"—and the shoe were found in a deserted barn about two miles from the scene of the abduction. McLellan got some backing from fellow cops who theorized that all the publicity had frightened Marion and she was afraid to disclose her whereabouts. But McLellan continued in full flight: "Although the boy, Jimmy Wilson, did not hit himself, there is more than one way to skin a cat. I am convinced the girl is somewhere in the province and that she is well. Further, I believe she went away of her own free will."

The chief's theory did not sit well with Ross McDowell, the grieving father. "I am convinced that if, by any chance, she is still alive, she is in the hands of some desperate monster who is afraid to let her go," he told the *Tely*. Day after day, he continued to trudge through the fields and thickets of Scarborough in a hopeless search. One day, "*The Telegram*'s radio-equipped helicopter" spotted McDowell making his way across a plowed field. It landed, picked him up, and, thereafter, made his search more efficient, if no more successful.

As Christmas approached, the whole McDowell story was beginning to slip into the back pages. Then, by a remarkable coincidence, her friend and deskmate at the engraving firm was murdered. Norma Schreiber, an attractive blonde, was found on the bed in her apartment, strangled. Her husband, Joseph, was charged with murder. Marion was back on Page One with a vengeance. Two "terror-stricken girls" at the engraving firm promptly fainted upon hearing the news about Norma. The firm's boss, Hubert B. Keenleyside, was understandably concerned: "I'm afraid of losing my staff here."

But police were unable to establish a link between the two events and, once again, Christmas and the rhythms of the news quieted the story down. But there was to be one more convulsion before the year ended. On December 29, the police revealed that Ross McDowell had received a crude ransom note, demanding $50,000 for Marion's return. It was a bit embarrassing for the *Tely*, but it was run, unedited, on Page One anyway.

Crudely printed and signed "THE KIDNAPPER" it read, in part: "This is not another joke being played on you. Your daughter is safe you can be sure. She has not telephoned like you said in the papers. She would do it if I would let her. I have always been a poor man. All I want for her is $50,000. When you have raised the money, let it be known in The Toronto Star. You see, I am very fussy. I read only The Toronto Star . . . ."

Chief McLellan concluded the note was "just another false

lead in a long line of false leads," and suggested McDowell forget about it. In fact, the cops, who had been intercepting McDowell's mail, grabbed the note before he saw it.

By now, winter had set in. There were no more clues, no more sensations. Billy Wilson went back to setting up his scaffolding. The McDowell family were finally left alone with their grief. Marion was well and truly gone.

But for the next eight months, there was sporadic talk at the Press Club, stories retold, a few paragraphs in the papers now and then when a Marion look-alike was reported in Buffalo or somewhere. Then Ian Paterson had his idea.

He passed it along to Art Cole, then the *Tely*'s city editor. Cole was enthusiastic and took it to MacFarlane. MacFarlane consulted John Bassett. The publisher loved the idea, but didn't think there was a chance of hooking Fabian of the Yard. But it was worth a try. He called Wally Reyburn, the *Tely*'s London columnist, and asked him to approach Fabian. Reyburn was dubious. "Fabian is a fabulous name in this country," he said. "He has other and bigger fish to fry."

Indeed, "the world's greatest detective" was a busy man. He had left his job as chief of Scotland Yard's Murder Squad for the much-better-paid glittering world of publishing and showbiz. Taking his casebook with him.

Robert Fabian had joined the constabulary in 1921. A tall, husky, good-looking and gregarious man, he was walking the beat only a short time before moving to the Vice Squad, with Soho as his parish. Two years later he was a detective, then on to Scotland Yard and to national recognition for a series of cases that had Fleet Street at his feet. They were fond of reciting his big ones, whenever he cracked another. One list went like this: The Wrotham Hill Murder—"A pretty girl strangled on a country road and Fabian of the Yard found the truck driver who 'didn't mean to pull the scarf so tight'"; The Black

Butterfly—"Her name was Mary Heath, but they called her The Black Butterfly at the cafe. Then her knifed body was found and Fabian had to find the gin bottle that was the key"; The Witch of Meon Hill—"The farmers of the Cotswold Hills called it witchcraft but Fabian called it murder"; The Deadly Pocket Handkerchief—"Someone was chloroforming girls on London streets—at least until Fabian found a man whose suit smelled of mothballs." And so on.

None the less, Fabian was the genuine article. A good cop who knew his parish and his villains, knew how helpful publicity could be and was relentless in pursuit of crime in the tight little underworld of London. He was also brave. In 1939, he calmly dismantled a bomb left in Piccadilly by Irish Nationalists. For that he was awarded the King's Medal for Gallantry (the police version of the Victoria Cross).

When Reyburn contacted him, he was in full showbiz flight. He had written his first book, *Fabian of the Yard*, a bestseller in England and abroad. A television series was being shown and a film had been done. But Fabian seemed ready for a break. Reyburn outlined the McDowell kidnapping and offered him $1,000 and expenses to come to Toronto and take it on. He asked for a day to think it over and then agreed. Why? "Two reasons," Fabian said. "First, it's the sort of case that would intrigue anybody. And second, I've always wanted to go to Canada."

Bassett was astonished and delighted. "He'll come for a thousand bucks? My God." Now, the *Tely*'s massive promotion department began to rev up—but in absolute secrecy. Ian Paterson and I were called into MacFarlane's office and told of the plan. I was stunned. So was Paterson. I was to be freed of other duties to handle Fabian. We would be given an office in the building and a suite at the Royal York. Paterson was to help with promotion. The *Star* would go nuts.

There was just one little thing, MacFarlane said. I had to get the man in charge of the McDowell case in Scarborough, Inspector of Detectives Harold Adamson, to come down to the paper that night so we could enlist his cooperation. Under no circumstances was I to tell him why he should visit the *Tely* in the middle of the night. Christ. Adamson and I got along all right. But we were by no means buddies. And he was one tough, stubborn sonovabitch when he wanted to be. But I would try.

Adamson was a remarkably dedicated cop. He looked like one. Big, laconic, handsome, he was seldom seen without his snap-brim fedora. He had joined the force as a police cadet and was working his way up. In later years he would become chief of the Toronto Police Force. Now, however, while he was doing most of the work on the McDowell case, Chief Wilf McLellan was doing most of the talking. A couple of other policemen from the provincial force, Detective Inspector Harold Graham and Detective Sergeant Norman Brickell, had also been helping out. When Fabian met them all later he would say, "These men reminded me of my former colleagues. Husky, able men. Thinkers."

"Harry," I said, that afternoon, "how would you like to come to the *Tely* with me tonight and meet some people?"

"Why?" Harry asked.

"I can't tell you."

"Piss off," said good old Harry.

I had no leverage. I knew a couple of things I hadn't written. There was the time the guy escaped from the Scarborough cells and, after a two-day township search, was discovered on the police-station roof. And a couple of his cowboys thought it was fun to pull up beside their pals on the highway and fire their revolvers in the air. But I had nothing serious.

It took all afternoon. But finally Adamson agreed. "It's a long road without a turning, Sears," he said, darkly. "You'd better not screw me."

When Adamson showed up at the office that night and the Fabian caper was explained to him, he was less than enthusiastic. He couldn't see what Fabian could do that the Scarborough police force and the Ontario Provincial Police force hadn't already done. Were we trying to put them down? A Scotland Yard cop coming in to show the rubes how it was done? Jeeeeezus. He didn't need to be told that the one thing he couldn't do, but Fabian could, was sell papers. He had already figured that out for himself. But, in the end, he agreed to at least talk to Fabian, not stand in his way and to keep his mouth shut until the world's greatest detective arrived. It was a practical decision. If Harry was going to make chief someday he didn't need to make an enemy of the *Tely*.

On Wednesday, August 11, 1954, Fabian's arrival was announced on the front page of *The Telegram*. All of the front page.

FABIAN OF THE YARD
ARRIVES IN TORONTO
TO LOOK FOR MARION

the two-inch headlines screamed. There was a huge picture of Fabian, striding along in a trenchcoat, pipe in hand. There was another picture of Marion McDowell. The modest little headline story read:

Robert Fabian—"Fabian of the Yard"—former chief of Scotland Yard's Murder Squad, is coming to Toronto to look for Marion McDowell.

The extraordinary sleuth, crack shot, Beau Brummell, champion boxer and certainly the world's greatest detective, has left London to fly to Canada.

Fabian of the Yard accepted the assignment to tackle the mystery of Marion's disappearance, at the suggestion of The Telegram. This newspaper invited him to attempt to break the case after Marion's father, Ross McDowell, appealed for another determined effort to relieve the anguish he and his wife have suffered for eight months.

Mr. McDowell, desperately anxious to end the awful uncertainty, turned to The Telegram. [A nice touch, that.]

This newspaper suggested an effort to interest the best detective on earth. Mr. McDowell agreed. After being given a summary of the case, Fabian of the Yard thought he could see "interesting possibilities for further investigation." He would take the job.

As soon as word was received that Fabian was coming to Toronto the wheels were set in motion to give him the status of a private detective in Ontario. Under the laws of the Province a private detective may not operate without a license from the Attorney General. [The wheels quickly got stuck. The AG's office was not having any of that nonsense. They gave Fabian a press pass.]

Scarboro police officials, while welcoming any assistance from anyone who might help them and obviously impressed at the calibre of the man who is coming here, said any official recognition of Fabian rested with the Attorney General.

As well as his fabulous experience, Fabian of the Yard brings a fresh approach to bear on the case, a mind free of any theories. He will be here by the end of the week.

Woweee. It was showtime.

When I was introduced to Fabian, I was impressed. He was fifty-three years old, a big, healthy, extrovert who spoke funny but was full of shrewd humor and insight. He bore, in retrospect, a remarkable resemblance to Edward Woodward, the star of television's *The Equalizer*. Fabian was perfectly clear about what he was to do: sell *Telegrams*. But he was also aware that he had a shot, a long one perhaps, of discovering what happened to Marion.

As he sat in his Royal York suite the first night, sipping Bassett's whiskey and talking, he explained that the best chance he had, the only chance really, was to stir up enough publicity to produce an informer, someone who knew something and, up to now, either didn't know he knew it or hadn't yet told.

He also knew he was walking delicate ground with the local police. "I have been rather a lone wolf myself at times," he said. "And jealous of my territory. Perhaps the Scarborough police are jealous of theirs. I'll just have to try and see if that little fellow who has so often walked beside me and given me a tip, can do it again."

The eight-month old trail was stone cold. Fabian had every confidence the local police had done all the necessary investigation. He had to establish a very high profile and then just . . . wait for a call.

I suggested that there should be two stories a day for the first while: I would write one news story about his investigation that day; and he and I would work together on a Fabian Report, which would appear under his signature. That seemed fine.

On Thursday, August 12, we let fly. The photography department had hoked up a picture of Bob—he was "Bob" now—peering out at the Toronto skyline from his hotel window with Marion's face floating just above a warehouse. The line story was the "warm welcome" the former superintendent of Scotland Yard had received from the Ontario Provincial Police. "We certainly welcome anyone who can help shed light on the mystery," said OPP Commissioner E.V. McNeill gamely.

The first Fabian Report began: "I hope my arrival here will not be taken in any wrong light. I'm not a psychic person. Not even a Sherlock Holmes. Just an ordinary bloke who has been invited by The Telegram to have a look into the Marion McDowell mystery. Don't be shy if you know anything . . . come and tell me."

Over on King Street, in the *Star* offices, there was considerable dismay. They had been thumped. How the hell could they cover Fabian's investigation when it was clearly a *Tely* promotion and Fabian wouldn't talk to them anyway? And that bastard Sears was probably going to be making it up.

But police ace Jocko Thomas rallied pretty quickly. The day after Fabian's spectacular arrival, the *Star*'s Page One story was headed: FABIAN WON'T FIND CLUES SHEDDING ANY NEW LIGHT ON MARION'S CASE, OPP SURE.

The story was a classic putdown:

> Robert Fabian is tackling the Marion McDowell mystery as a private citizen. The former crack detective of Scotland Yard who has turned to writing and television was not licensed as a private detective when he applied at the office of Commander E.V. McNeill of the Ontario Provincial Police yesterday. He was refused.
>
> Fabian's work will be a "simple, routine checking of the case," OPP Insp. Harold Graham said. "He will get the cooperation that we would accord to anyone else who had the experience he has had," said Chief. Insp. W.J. Franks. "If Mr. McDowell, the father of the girl, had similar experience he would be able to get the same help that we will give Mr. Fabian and the same goes for others."

A second *Star* story said Fabian's arrival will produce "a deluge of reports which will confuse the case even more, police predicted."

We knew we had them by the short and curlies. So did they.

Fabian had been set up in the office of a *Telegram* executive who was ill. He had a phone and a secretary. We fell into a routine pretty quickly. Each day he advertised that he would be by the phone for two hours—please call. The rest of the time, he and I, in a chauffeured limo, would wander about Scarborough or the red-light district or the vicinity of the Don Jail, setting up pictures for the next day. In the evening we would retire to his hotel suite, pour a couple of Scotches, order in steaks and invent the stories for tomorrow's edition. It was grand fun.

Frequently a *Star* car would follow us about, so we charged around, speeding up, slowing down, keeping mysterious appointments. There wasn't a damn thing they could write until our first edition came out.

By the second day, the circulation of the *Tely* had jumped 60,000. At the end of the caper, we held on to 10,000.

There was, however, one problem. Fabian, by the end of the first week, was no closer to finding out what happened to Marion, and a tiny bit of tension was beginning to build. How the hell were we going to get out of this thing without a kidnapper?

We were steadily getting more inventive. Bob decided to introduce white slavers, always a seller, only to rule them out. "I think we can all clear from your minds the thought that this was the kidnapping of a girl for the sensational reason of leading her to prostitution," he dictated. "He certainly wouldn't bother to tear a girl away from her escort. I have seen many unaccompanied young ladies who would be far easier prey. I've received a number of letters suggesting that Marion was the victim of white slavers who had taken her over the border. I think we can dismiss this entirely." That seemed to do it for white slavers whom, as far as I knew, no one had ever suspected before.

All this shameless exploitation, the McDowell family endured with calm and dignity. While Fabian met them from time to time, I did not. They continued to hope that all this publicity would flush out the kidnapper. Or perhaps, Marion.

But now things were really getting a bit anxious. People kept asking if Fabian was getting anywhere. "It's a natural question," Bob wrote in one of his reports, "and I don't mind a bit answering it. Yes. But I can hardly be expected to enlarge on it." Which was a good thing.

He came up with a carnival muscle man whom Marian had apparently dated, and a boyfriend who wanted to marry her and had threatened to kill her if she didn't agree. The McDowell family must have been increasingly astonished at their daughter's colorful social life. One visitor said he knew who Marion's assailant was and supplied a description that could have fitted half the men in Toronto. But we ran a picture of the informer anyway. It was a shot of a copy boy, I think, with his face entirely painted out.

"Okay," said Bob, at the end of the second week, "I've got to see Wilson, can't stall any longer." He'd already been in touch with the kid's family and Jimmy said he was ready to talk to Fabian whenever he wanted.

So, on the first day of September, Jimmy came around to the hotel for a chat. Fabian had prepared a sheet with about fifty questions for him to answer. There was no doubt that Wilson was the key to the case. He had been hammered day after day by the cops. But he never wavered. He had been hit. He was knocked out. He saw Marion carried off and put in the trunk of someone's car. But there were still some curious features. Jimmy said the man had demanded money and had taken his wallet. It was found nearby with the money inside.

Fabian questioned him for hours. I don't think he got anywhere. But he insisted we put in his report: "The picture of what happened that night has come into perfect focus in my mind. And although I am not in a position to make a prediction I feel, as footballers in England say, 'I'm shaping my feet for a shot at the goal.'" Jimmy told him he thought Marion was still alive. Fabian couldn't agree. He was convinced he was investigating a murder.

Matters were quickly coming to a showdown. Fabian had done just about everything he could. Milked everything, anyway.

His television series was running on a local station and his movie was showing at five Toronto theaters. It was time to wind things up. But how?

"I suppose I could do the old 'I now know who the murderer is but I cannot reveal his name because there is not enough evidence to convict him' lark," he mused. I didn't think that was such a hot idea. He finally settled on the "I must go home, but I'll be back" ploy.

He phoned Ross McDowell and told him he had to get back to London. He was sorry he hadn't been able to do anything.

Fabian and I wrote his last report on September 6. He began it: "To Mr. Ross McDowell and The Telegram. I submit for your information an interim report on the investigations I have made into the mysterious disappearance of the evening of 6th December, 1953, of Marion Joan McDowell, aged 17 years . . . ."

It was all supposed to sound dreadfully official but later on Fabian offered his own assessment, not of the case, but of Marion.

"A lot has been said about Marion but I know that fundamentally she was a good girl. [We were back to that at the end.] Wild and restless, agreed, but she was at the age so difficult in the youth of today. . . . Admonish them and they flare up. Let them run, they look upon you as a fool. They know . . . or do they?

"She sought the company of young cafe loungers, pin table scroungers and street corner loafers. As opportunity came she threw herself at youths who owned motorcycles. She loved speed and throughout it all she was a popular girl . . . perhaps too popular."

Fabian said Ross McDowell thought himself responsible for not keeping a tighter rein on Marion. "To him I say 'It might have happened to Marion had she been a teacher at Sunday School.'"

He recorded that throughout the inquiry he had travelled 2,354 miles, had personally seen 52 people at the office and 22 outside. He had received 587 letters and dealt with 920 telephone calls. In every way, the *Tely* had got its money's worth.

Fabian returned to London, completing what surely was the premier newspaper crime promotion of the decade. But not the only one.

While every paper in the country competed in the crime-and-violence market, the only newspaper rivals that could match the *Star* and the *Tely* for mixing blood and ink were the Vancouver *Sun* and *The Province*.

The Province was the top paper in Vancouver and *The Sun* fought for decades to catch up. As Managing Editor Hal Straight said: "What we tried to do in *The Sun* was to get something that *The Province* didn't have. To do that you had to have real, lively, energetic people, which is why the second papers made the great reporters. They loved it, they just loved it. Your big problem was to get them not to try too hard and cheat a little bit and not tell the right story."

In the fifties, however, *The Province* had the liveliest staffer of all. His name was Ray Munro and he was a photographer-reporter.

"Compared to him," recalls Canadian Press editor Charlie Bruce, "Hildy Johnson of *The Front Page* was a choir boy."

Bruce tells of one early Munro caper that still lives in legend.

"In the spring and summer of 1949 the secluded quiet of Stanley Park had become unsafe for lovers. Night-time marauders made its byways sinister with the hazards of robbery and rape. Police were handicapped—short of men and faced with reluctance by victims to tell what happened.

"Munro conceived the idea of setting out a decoy. Reporter Don McClean, a slightly built RCAF veteran, borrowed a red wig. In Munro's car the two embarked on an enterprise that had, as *The Province* said in a resulting picture caption, elements of both Keystone Cops and *Charley's Aunt*.

"A preliminary run produced nothing. The next night Munro and McClean tried again. Near Brockton Point they began to feign a spooning session in dim moonlight. Beside Munro in the driver's seat lay an automatic. McClean clutched a borrowed policeman's billy. The right-hand door of the car flew open. A light flashed in their faces. A voice said: 'This is the morality squad.' McClean swung his billy against a head. Munro dived over him at the man behind the light.

"In September the captive, a Port Coquitlam laborer, drew a year for impersonating police. In November, after a victim of an April attack had testified, he started a fifteen-year prison term for rape."

The Province, of course, was exultant over the bizarre capture. The story nearly filled the front page. But *The Sun* barely sniffed: "Two citizens catch robbery suspect."

The Province had another remarkable exclusive some years later. A prisoner at Oakalla prison had taken a guard hostage and was holding a razor at his throat. He said his case was a frameup and he wanted his story in the paper as a condition of releasing the guard. *The Province* agreed and reporter Bruce Larsen went into the prison to talk to him. *The Province* printed an extra with the banner head: THIS STORY FOR A LIFE. It won Larsen a National Newspaper Award. The prisoner got an extra year on his twenty-year sentence.

Crime is no longer the story it was in the fifties. A shame, perhaps, for readers. Sometimes at night, decades later, I muse that one day a man and woman will walk into my office and say: "Mr. Sears, my name is Ross McDowell and this is my daughter, Marion. . . . "

Our hero at 24 years when the Great Newspaper War began.
CANADA WIDE

The Telegram, *the Old Lady of Melinda Street, in her glory days.*
METRO TORONTO LIBRARY/BALDWIN ROOM

Top left: Telegram *publisher,*
John Bassett, circa 1952, when he took
over the underdog newspaper.
MILNE STUDIO/TORONTO STAR

Top right: Borden Spears, managing
editor of the Star *in the fifties and*
a great newspaperman.
TORONTO STAR

MARILYN'S STORY

'I FELT I WAS SWIMMING FOREVER

SATURDAY Cloudy, Cooler Low 35 High 66 Details Page Two	CO-COL. 79TH YEAR	## THE TELEGRAM	The Pink Tely **Night**
	56 PAGES	TORONTO, FRIDAY, SEPTEMBER 10, 1954	PRICE 5 CENTS	Final Sports—Markets

THE PICTURE YOU'VE BEEN WAITING FOR...

(SEVEN DRAMATIC PAGES OF PICTURES AND STORIES: 2, 3, 5, 9, 12, 19 AND 29)

'Your Mind Goes Blank And You Just Keep Going'

Marilyn Bell

'I haven't got a stomach' was the fir—' thing I said to my trainer, Gus Ryder, when they pulled me into th. oat. At least that's what he says I said. I don't remember. I know i wasn't sick but I felt as f my stomach wasn't there.

I feel terrific now. All I want to do is sleep. And eat. The doctor ays I've probably lost 20 pounds, not eating for—how many hours is t since I've eaten anyway? About 24? It feels like more than that.

They gave me syrup and pablum out in the lake. I think I stopped twice for syrup the last few minutes It's hard to remember now and it's hard to explain how I feel. They say I went to sleep twice. Maybe I did but I know I kept right on swimming.

It was the darkness and the eels that bothered me most. It was so dark that first night. I called to the boat to turn all its lights on so I could see something. They did and I felt better. But the eels kept coming around me. I could feel them. One of them fastened on my leg. I could feel its sucking mouth. It slowed me a little and finally I kicked it off.

THOSE LAST TWO HOURS

The last two hours were the hardest. I felt like I did in Atlantic City when I swam the 26-mile marathon there—as if I'd been swimming all my life. Every time I brought my head up I saw the same old things, the sky, the waves and the darkness of the water again. Even though you have boats there you seem to be so alone. You

See MY STORY, Page 2

A Victory Cavalcade For Marilyn Tonight

Marilyn Bell, New Toronto's 16-year-old high school girl who swam her heart out yesterday in the most gruelling test of swimming endurance ever recorded, is a national heroine today.

This afternoon it was learned that she swam with a strained tendon in her left ankle constantly in pain—yet never telling her coach.

And tonight the city she fought her way 40 miles across wave-tossed Lake Ontario to reach, will hail her with a giant victory celebration.

In a radio broadcast today Marilyn thanked "all the Canadians who were pulling for me. It was a great help."

"Without them I could not have done it," she said.

A Bar st. ticker tape parade originally planned for today, by City Hall officials, has been postponed until noon Monday.

When she is received by the Mayor on the City Hall steps, Marilyn will be presented with a set of matched luggage for her recent accomplishment in Atlantic City.

In addition, the city will present her with a second and more valuable gift, probably jewelry for swimming Lake Ontario.

A cavalcade of boats will

bear a triumphant Marilyn for a mile-and-a-half along the waterfront, inside the seawall,

to the CNE grounds at 7 p.m. There at the Bandshell, the *See HEROINE, Page 10*

Where To See Her Today

7.00 p.m.—HMCS York, where boats will pick up Marilyn for a victory cavalcade along the waterfront.

7.45 p.m.—CNE Bandshell, where Marilyn will receive a presentation. Broadcast on CJBC. Rebroadcast on CBL at 8.30 p.m.

And during the evening CNE Grandstand performances when she will make a personal appearance.

Ticker tape parade postponed until noon Monday.

Toronto M-H Union To Strike Tonight

Toronto branch of Master Harris Ferguson Ltd. King st. will strike at midnight.

This announcement was made for George Burt, Canadian director of CIO-CCL United Automobile Workers Union after a last-ditch negotiating session this morning.

Three thousand employes will be affected.

The meeting was to get the company to extend its contract termination deadline to the end

of the month to give union ne gotiators a chance to discuss the issure with the international executive board of the union in Detroit.

The board is scheduled to *See STRIKE, Page 5*

Woodbine Results See Race Page — Page 34

'We Prayed For Her Success'

"I stopped praying for protection and started praying for success."

These were the words of Mother Yvonne of Loretto College School where Marilyn Bell is a pupil.

"Throughout the day the staff and pupils followed closely our Marilyn's progress. We prayed long and sincerely for her protection," Mother Yvonne said.

"But I am afraid that near the end when I heard she was tiring, I prayed for success."

Marilyn's Tired Left Hand Just Touches Sloping Edge Of Breakwater As Tely Camera Catches Exclusive Picture Of Her Epic Swim

Page One of the Tely, September 10, 1954, featured a sensational picture of Marilyn completing her swim, and a controversial signature.

CANADA WIDE

Marilyn Bell struggles toward Toronto with Star reporter George Bryant (left) and coach Gus Ryder in boat.
CANADA WIDE

Gallant Shirley Campbell is interviewed at waterside.
CITY OF TORONTO ARCHIVES/GLOBE AND MAIL

16 Pages of Color Comics

WEEKEND TELY
Combined With

10¢

SUNDAY
Cloudy. Cool
Low 40
High 55
Details Page Two   DIM OUTLOOK   79TH YEAR

THE TELEGRAM

TORONTO, SATURDAY, OCTOBER 16, 1954

102 PAGES

The Pink Tely
Night
Final Sports—Markets

FEAR 71 DROWNED
300 MISSING IN THIS AREA
CITY BLOCKED OFF

Heroism of one of Toronto's finest nearly costs him his life as P.C. Richard Stock is saved from Humber River just after man drowned

I Saw A Man Drown . . .

By VAL SEARS
Telegram Staff Reporter

I saw one man drown.

At least as far as the police and I could tell he drowned. We never saw him again.

I was in the Weston police station last night when a call came in that "the dead are floating down the river."

Two police cruisers loaded with officers and civilians headed for the Lawrence ave. bridge across the Humber River where we thought we might stop some of the survivors. My car was right behind.

We raced to the partially destroyed bridge. With flashlights and lamps we watched the swirling muddy water carry parts of houses and trees down with terrific speed.

I heard a muffled scream. I spun around to the other side of the bridge. Then it came again. With our lamps

CLINGS TO BUSH
Loses grip, then swept away

we could see an elderly man clinging to a fallen tree branch almost in the middle of the river.

He was screaming: "Help me. Save me."

The police and firemen ran for ropes.

Then a young policeman stripped off his tunic and shoes. He was later identified as PC Richard Stock of Toronto City Police.

"Don't go in," his fellow officers yelled at him. "You'll never make it. You'll drown in that torrent."

PC Stock ignored the shouts. He slipped into the racing water and, shouting encouragement to the man, began swimming and pulling himself along on tree branches.

Suddenly, the elderly man disappeared.

Just as suddenly, PC Stock lost his grip on the tree

See DROWNS, Page 12

$100 Million Loss
Province May Aid

The death toll continued to climb late this afternoon amidst chaotic confusion following the ravages of Hurricane Hazel.

At 5 p.m. 71 persons were drowned or presumed drowned. Another eight died in accidents caused by the storm.

All but five of the drowning victims were in the Toronto area.

Three hundred are still missing and damage may reach one hundred million dollars.

A provincial and civic emergency has been declared. Toronto is virtually cut off from its suburbs by wild waters.

Metro Chairman Fred Gardiner ordered the city blocked off to all but essential travel. Only two bridges now carry traffic over the Humber River, and police are turning back all cars which are not on emergency missions.

The Provincial Government is considering financial aid for the Toronto area.

Welfare Minister W. A. Goodfellow said he was "very greatly concerned and watching the situation very closely." The province set a precedent when it shared the costs of storm damage caused by the Sarnia tornado.

The early estimate of the death toll was trebled shortly after noon today. This is the breakdown:

Raymore dr., Etobicoke—six known drowned, 24 believed drowned.

Etobicoke Creek—two women drowned.

Old Mill Bridge—five Etobicoke firemen drowned when they were swept from their fire truck during a rescue attempt; body of another man recovered.

Weston—one drowned, four believed drowned.

See STORM, Page 2

Storm Victims

KNOWN DEAD:
Bob Radley, 7, Clarence st., Woodbridge.
Diane Radley, 9, Clarence st., Woodbridge.
Mrs. Donald Reid, 29, of Woodbridge.
Mrs. Eddie Curtis, 20 Fairview ave., Weston.
Stewart Nicholson, Etobicoke.

See VICTIMS, Page 2

FOOTBALL
BIG FOUR

ARGOS . . .	6	6	6	9	27
OTTAWA . .	0	5	6	0	11
MONTREAL..	0	11	18	17	46
HAMILTON..	0	0	10	1	11

COLLEGE UNION

VARSITY . .	0	0	0	0	0
QUEEN'S . . .	0	18	0	2	20
McGILL . .	6	0	0	0	6
WESTERN . .	6	12	1	6	25

See Sports Page 26 for Stories

IN THE TELEGRAM TO-DAY

About New Canadians—23
Amusements—18 to 20
Billy Graham—34
Births, Marriages, Deaths—34
Book Page—33
Building, Real Estate—12
Business, Finance—29, 30
Church Notices—14 to 16
Classified Ads—34 to 42
Comics—43, 44
"Double-Take"—22
Editorials—6
Fox Farm—18
Khaki and Blue—45
Let's Explore Your Mind—43
Locke Dollson—41
Margaret Aitken—10
McNamara's Bandwagon—18
Medical Roundup—12
News of Ontario—33

Men o' the World—8
Radio and TV—8
Schooner Days—8
See-Hear—8
Sports—26 to 28
Tele Hobby Page—
Thomas Richard Henry—6
Travel—31
Up Modoela Way—6
Waterfront—20
Women's Page—10, 11
Your Garden—9
Your Horoscope—10

Comic Dictionary
DIVORCE
A legal device that prevents you from keeping a good cook even if you marry her.

Bar Sightseers
CNR 'If Asked' To Run Specials

With Toronto still shut off west and north police refused to look any farther ahead than "tonight's traffic."

Etobicoke police, who have stopped all traffic on Bloor and Dundas in both directions, said they hoped to have the Dundas bridge open tonight.

"We're working on it," said a spokesman.

Asked whether persons who work in Toronto should try to get in tomorrow morning, he said: "We haven't even started thinking about that."

Meanwhile police hinted motorists who flock to the devastated districts on "sightseeing tours" might have their cars impounded.

Efforts are being made to open the Humber with a Bailey bridge tonight but success depends on flood moderation.

Canadian National Railways would be willing to supply special

See WASH OUTS, Page 4

Page One, October 16, 1954, when tragedy blew in to Toronto.
CANADA WIDE

The Humber River at Scarlett Road in the aftermath of Hurricane Hazel.
CANADA WIDE

A drowning man clings to a branch in the Humber River as Hazel rips through Toronto.
CANADA WIDE

THE TELEGRAM

BOYD, KILLER PALS LOOSE
POLICE 'SHOOT ON SIGHT'
HUSBAND "WON'T BE TAKEN ALIVE"--MRS. BOYD

Used Card Game
As Escape Front
Dummies In Cots

Edwin Boyd and Co. used card games as a front for sawing their way out of the Don Jail, police learned today as the trail of Canada's four most-wanted men grew fainter hour by hour.

The objects of Toronto's greatest manhunt—two accused murderers and two bank bandits—stood on a card table to saw through the bars of their Death Row window, police learned.

They stood on this same card table to wiggle through the 13½ by 9¼-inch opening and make a clean getaway overnight.

Late this afternoon 2,000 police, with "shoot on sight" orders, had no clear idea of the whereabouts of:

1. EDWIN ALONZO BOYD, MASTER BANK BANDIT, AND BRAINS OF THE ESCAPE;

2. LEONARD JACKSON, ACCUSED OF MURDERING A TORONTO POLICEMAN, AND WHO IS MINUS HIS ARTIFICIAL FOOT TODAY;

3. STEVE SUCHAN, JOINTLY CHARGED WITH JACKSON IN THE MURDER OF SGT. OF DETS. EDMUND TONG;

4. WILLIAM RUSSELL JACKSON, ANOTHER BANK ROBBER AND A TWO-TIME JAILBREAKER.

For three—Boyd and the two Jacksons—it was the second successful escape from the matchbox-like Don Jail.

WIFE DOUBTS BOYD TAKEN ALIVE

Mrs. Boyd told a Telegram reporter she didn't think her husband would be taken alive this time.

Mayor Lamport said back from his Lake Simcoe cottage, termed the break "Toronto's greatest shame," and senior police officials, disgusted and bitter, called it "a disgrace to Canada."

Said one: "It has made the Toronto Jail and the City Police a laughing stock to criminals."

A reward of $8,000—$2,000 per head—was offered promptly by the Provincial Government. Attorney General Dana Porter announced it without comment.

Mayor Lamport said the city would match the reward, bringing the total to $4,000 on the head of each wanted man, or $16,000. In addition, the Canadian Bankers' Association is expected to issue a special reward.

Pictures of the desperadoes were flashed on television over CBC station CBLT, thus bringing the new medium into play in Canadian crime for the first time.

First reports indicated that a guard had looked in on the second-floor group of four cells at 5 a.m. and pronounced "everything OK." But police have been grilling this guard, and it is said the escape may have taken place much earlier.

Con. David Balfour, who inspected the four adjoining cells, declared that "they had definitely not been slept in."

It was evident, however, that the four let themselves out of their cells—or were let out—by means of a key. The cells had not been tampered with. But the bars on the window opening onto the common corridor had been hacked through.

The sawing of the bars—two on the inside, two more on the outside—had been a painstaking job, investigators said. It had taken many hours, perhaps as long as a week. And

See BOYD ESCAPE, Page 3

GUNS READY
Police hunt desperadoes

Edwin Alonzo Boyd—Age 37; height 5 feet 8 inches; medium build; dark brown hair; blue eyes; medium complexion; four front teeth false in upper jaw.

Steve Suchan—Age 24; height 5 feet 10 inches; medium build; brown hair; brown eyes; medium complexion; good teeth; lower half of face pimply.

William Russell Jackson—Age 37; height 5 feet 7¼ inches; medium build; brown hair; blue eyes; medium complexion; poor teeth, has name "Eleanor" tattooed on right forearm.

Leonard Jackson—Age 29; height 5 feet 10 inches; medium build; dark brown hair; brown eyes; good teeth; left foot off, limps slightly, has artificial foot, scar over left eye.

OFFICIAL POLICE DESCRIPTION OF WANTED MEN

Page One, September 8, 1952, reflects the excitement the Boyd Gang's exploits precipitated.

CANADA WIDE

Edwin Alonzo Boyd is captured (once). Left to right: Mayor Alan Lamport,
Detective Adolphus Payne, Boyd, Detective Jack Kenneth.
CANADA WIDE

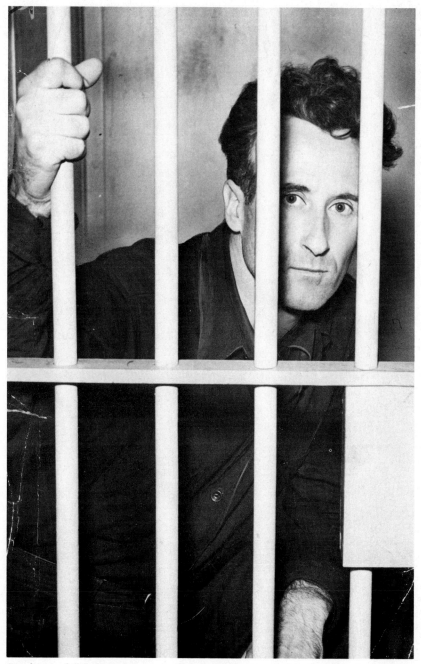

Boyd peers defiantly at the camera from behind bars at the North York police station.
CANADA WIDE

A crowd gathers around the North York barn where the Boyd gang was captured minutes earlier.
CITY OF TORONTO ARCHIVES/GLOBE AND MAIL

Our hero confers with Fabian of the Yard (center) and Ross McDowell, father of the kidnapped girl.
CANADA WIDE

THURSDAY
Getting Dull
Low 50
High 70
Details Page Two

DIM OUTLOOK 79TH YEAR   42 PAGES   TORONTO, WEDNESDAY, AUGUST 11, 1954   PRICE 5 CENTS

THE TELEGRAM

FABIAN OF THE YARD ARRIVES IN TORONTO TO LOOK FOR MARION

World's Greatest Detective Tackles Kidnap Mystery

Robert Fabian—"Fabian of the Yard"—former chief of Scotland Yard's murder squad, has come to Toronto to look for Marion Mc-Dowell.

The extraordinary sleuth, crack shot, Beau Brummell, champion boxer and, certainly, the world's greatest detective, arrived here today.

Fabian of the Yard accepted the assignment to tackle the mystery of Marion's disappearance, at the suggestion of The Telegram. This newspaper invited him to attempt to break the case after Marion's father, Ross McDowell, appealed for another determined effort to relieve the anguish he and his wife have suffered for eight months.

Mr. McDowell, desperately anxious to end the awful uncertainty, turned to The Telegram.

This newspaper suggested an effort to interest the best detective on earth.

Mr. McDowell agreed. And The Telegram immediately had its London columnist, Wallace Reyburn, invite Superintendent Fabian to accept the assignment.

Fabian of the Yard was given a summary of the case. After an examination of the facts he thought he could see "interesting possibilities for further investigation." He would take on the job.

In less than a week his flight to Canada and to Toronto was arranged.

As soon as word was received that Fabian was coming to Toronto the wheels were set in motion to give him the status of a private detective in Ontario. Under the laws of the Province a private detective may not operate without license from the Attorney General.

Scarboro police officials, while welcoming any assistance from anyone who might help them and obviously impressed at the calibre of the man who is coming here, said any official recognition of Fabian rested with the Attorney General.

As well as his fabulous experience, Fabian of the Yard brings to bear on the case a mind free of any theories. His fresh approach to the mystery may well give him an advantage over those intimately connected with the investigation since Marion's disappearance last Dec. 6.

Marion McDowell: Still Missing In Baffling Kidnap Mystery

Fleeing Gunman Wounds Jeweler

A gunman who shot Douglas Johnson, 32, son of the proprietor of Johnson's Jewelery store in the leg during a vain holdup attempt today, escaped through heavy crowds in the old afternoon.

Police were combing the area for no man who just after firing a second shot at proprietor J. W. Johnson as he grabbed for an iron bar.

Nothing was stolen.

Police said late today they expected an arrest within 'a very short time.'

The gunman was chased through the crowd on the street by Kirk Johnson, another son of the proprietor.

Rushed to St. Michael's Hospital, Douglas Johnson was reported suffering loss of blood and shock, but was not in serious condition.

Both Johnsons and a customer were in the store when the holdup man walked in, pulling a long black revolver from

under his coat, pointed it at: Douglas and ordered him to hand over his money.

When the clerk didn't move fast enough he fired, hitting
See GUNMAN, Page 16

Both Sides To Hear PM In Rail Row

Ottawa, Aug. 11—(CP)—Prime Minister St. Laurent announced today that representatives of the railways and non-operating unions have accepted a cabinet invitation to confer here tomorrow with the government on the rail strike issue.

Mr. St. Laurent made the announcement after a cabinet meeting.

He said tomorrow's conference will be between himself and Labor Minister Gregg and representatives of the railways and the general negotiating committee of the unions.

Earlier today, the unions accepted St. Laurent's
See RAIL, Page 3

Boy, 6, Drowns By Crowded Dock

Peterboro, Aug. 11—(Special)—A six-year-old boy slipped unnoticed from a crowded dock on Stoney Lake near here and drowned today. He was Ted Carveth, son of Mr. and Mrs. Ross Carveth of Peterboro.

FORT ERIE RESULTS

(Fort Erie Story and Other Results on Tely Race Page)

FIRST RACE—(Off 2.00)

CAPTAIN BELL (Roy) 73.40 34.00 15.60
SILENT HONOR (Davern) 13.10 9.40
BYATES SENIOR (Duprey) 6.40
abBONVIVUS (CC Brown) 4.40
   Time 1.46 4-5. Seth Bull, Chance Tous, General Sam, Sha Fire, Greystone, Eric's Boy, Fair Offer. (Euphoria. fClemia, fLorna D. also ran. dh—Dead heat for third. f—Field.

SECOND RACE—(Off 2.30)

GALLANT BLUE (Walker) 8.70 5.80 3.70
MANTOLI (L. Gonzalez) 9.00 6.50
CHIC BLUE (C. Brown) 5.20
   Time 1.20 2-5. Mr. Why, On The Air, Bitterroot, Fair Mark, Harry L., Tring Fair, Sallingaway, Barbi's Joe, Harvey M. also ran.
   Double—Captain Bell and Gallant Blue paid $373.20.

THIRD RACE—(Off 3.02)

aBIG STORM (Walker) 7.20 3.40 2.60
SURE QUIS (Davern) 4.10 3.20
HASTY DREAM (Oyeyama) 4.70
   Time 1.08. aTamarack Bay, Rule of Mine, Blencrest, Isacasey, Teddy Lure, Another Step also ran.
   a—Stafford Farms entry.

FOURTH RACE—(Off 3.36)

BONIBOYLE (Albert) 13.80 5.90 5.00
WINGING HOME (Behrens) 5.90 4.30
AFLAME (Wholey) 5.60
   Time 1.14 . aMarys Pal, aAssert, Howard Dear. Please Pat, Her Chance, Bureaucrat, Silver Blossom, Munda's Tuppy also ran. a—Merrill and McCorrick entry.

FIFTH RACE—(Off 4.66)

ABEDINA (Johnson) 5.80 3.20 2.80
HOITY TOITY (Behrens) 3.40 2.70
GAMBOGE (Pederson) 3.40
   Time 1.20. Flying Pebble, My Wind, Rip Luck, High Value, Bright Head also ran.

SIXTH RACE (Off 4.35)

KANDI KID (C. Brown) 12.50 5.90 4.30
WAR GENERAL (Johnson) 4.80 3.20
CLIPPER B. (Lindberg) 3.10
   Time. 1.11 4-5. Vivace, Setalor, War Booty, Paytu also ran.

"Fabian Of The Yard" Steps In At The Telegram's Request

Close-Up Of Fabian...

By IAN PATERSON
Telegram Staff Reporter

Who is Robert Fabian—Fabian of the Yard?

He is a spruce, hard-muscled five feet 10 inches of methodical energy. He has won a coveted badge of courage and a solid reputation as the world's greatest detective.

Officially he is ex-Detec-

tive Superintendent Robert Fabian, former chief of Scotland Yard's murder squad. In Britain his name is as well known as Sherlock Holmes.

He is a relentless policeman who has won not only the fear but the respect of criminals.

In 1939 he calmly dismantled a crudely-made

bomb left in Piccadilly by Irish Nationalists. For that he was awarded the King's Medal for Gallantry (the police V.C.).

In the same drawer where he keeps that medal is a bronze medallion. It was presented to him in a bar by a group of London's most notorious underworld
See CLOSEUP, Page 2

Long Battle Won

Epilepsy Shorn Of Its Terrors

By MRS. L. B.

My return home was the beginning of a new life. The Christmas tree, long barren of smell, was gaily decorated and lighted. With it my girlish smile, but the love, comfort and encouragement or family adjustments could have been difficult. My worst struggle was the own lack of confidence. Every attack is a slight setback in this respect. Convulsions persisted in a mild way, my diary showing an average of six in eight a month in the first eight months after my hospitalization, but as time wore on they became fewer and farther apart. Looking back over the nine years since the first grim days of my illness, one would almost believed me cured, for I may now go many months, even a year without an attack.

An epileptic sufferer who at one point seemed on the brink of death or the insane asylum, Mrs. L. B. tells the final, moving instalment of her story today.

This third and final article will give inspiration to other epileptics.

Epilepsy holds little terror for me, for I am well acquainted with this sly fellow who was once my complete master. I have an accurate way to trump his every trick, but must be forever watchful, for he is a relentless adversary. I have learned the things he thrives on, these I withhold, in that way "skinning my ref.ness. But he has proven of great help to me.
See EPILEPSY, Page 3

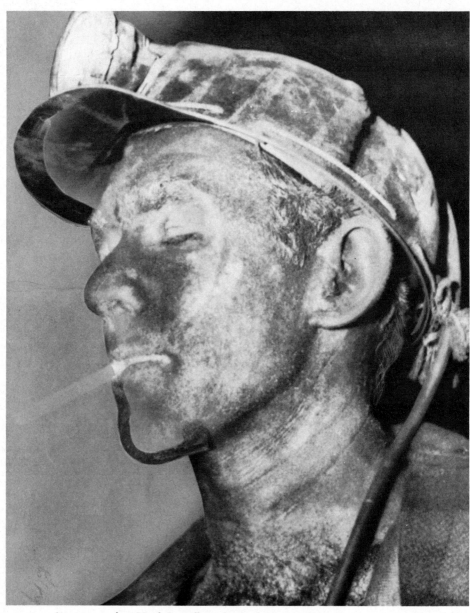

A rescue worker, Hugh Langille, exhausted after searching for survivors in the collapsed Springhill mine.

TORONTO STAR

Rescue Draegermen, their air equipment still on, grab coffee after coming out of the poisoned darkness of the Springhill mine.
CANADA WIDE

The old Metropole hotel in Toronto, where lawyer Arthur Maloney held court for reporters, friends and rogues.
METRO TORONTO LIBRARY/BALDWIN ROOM

Lawyer Dave Humphrey, the great entertainer of the criminal bar.
TORONTO STAR

Lawyer Arthur Maloney, advocate and bon vivant, considers a defence.
TORONTO STAR

5 | The Lady of the Lake

The kid was halfway across the lake before the *Tely* woke up. By then the cars were beginning to back up along Lakeshore Road, their radios on, people staring out across the choppy water of Lake Ontario. And an old lady was down by the shore, murmuring over and over: "C'mon, little girl . . . C'mon little girl . . . "

That's when Doug MacFarlane, the managing editor of the *Tely*, realized he had trouble, bad, bad trouble. Three women were trying to swim across Lake Ontario, two of them professional marathon swimmers—no problem. But the third was a sixteen-year-old girl from Toronto. And she, for heaven's sake, was leading. Already one of the professionals had been pulled out, sick, and the other, after a bad start, was way behind.

Marilyn Bell was heading for home—maybe the first person to swim the lake, ever. And the *Star*, the goddamn *Star*, had her tied up, a man in the boat beside her with a contract in his pocket for her exclusive story.

It was not, thought MacFarlane, cursing, that the *Tely* couldn't have had her first. Weeks before, the girl's coach,

Gus Ryder, from the Lakeshore Swim Club, had called on John Bassett, the publisher of *The Telegram*, and said he thought his girl could swim the thirty-two miles across Lake Ontario. Would the *Tely* be interested in sponsoring her for the $5,000 they needed for expenses?

Bassett, who knew Ryder was a marvelous coach and a swimming instructor for crippled children, said: "Gus, a sixteen-year-old girl, swimming Lake Ontario? The *Tely* can't be part of that. It's not the money . . . but it's cruelty to children. In any event, you'll have to pull her out half-way across. No, Gus, I can't do it."

So Ryder went up the street to the *Star* and got the money.

Now, out there, stroking a steady fifty beats a minute, up to the top of one wave, down the other, her stomach aching and lamprey eels sucking at her thighs, Marilyn Bell was coming to Toronto. She was terribly weary; the skyline never seemed to get any closer. Her eyes were red and her brain was fogged. But her legs fluttered in rhythm and her arms kept moving, up and over, up and over. . . . She had been preparing for this forever it seemed. She would not quit.

Once, a long time ago, before the rivers leading to the lake were poisoned by industrial greed, when the shore itself was open and clean, Toronto was attached to the water and famed around the world for water sportsmen. The oarsman Ned Hanlan had been champion of the world, followed by the huge sculler from Orillia, Jake Gaudaur. By the twenties, the marathon swimmers had taken over the waterfront—George Young, with his barrel chest, who went on, a lonely Canadian, to be the first to conquer the channel between Catalina Island and the mainland in an incredible swim; Ernst Vierkoetter, The Black Shark of Germany; then Margaret Ravior, Martha Norelius and up to Cliff Lumsdon and Tom Park, the current marathon champions.

But by now, in September 1954, marathon swimming had

faded from the front page. The Canadian National Exhibition still, off and on, sponsored a marathon inside the breakwater at the CNE waterfront. But hockey, football, tennis, whatever, had swept the swimmers away.

Still, Marilyn Bell had been swimming all her life. It was her life. Born in Toronto on October 19, 1937, the daughter of an accounting clerk, Sydney, and his wife, Grace, Marilyn had been a Dolphinette at age nine. She was slightly built but strong. And, best of all, she had heart. In her first race outside of a warm pool, she did a one-mile swim in icy, choppy Lake Ontario. Beaten by the cold, she finished swimming on her back. But she finished.

"That's the way to swim, kid, finish a race if you can," said a woman, waiting with a towel. It was Winnie Roach Leuszler, the marathon pro, whom Marilyn would go up against in the lake swim seven years later.

But her father knew she needed better coaching. So he arranged for her to attend the Lakeshore Swim Club where her coach would be Gus Ryder. Ryder was a coaching legend in Toronto, not only for the champions he turned out, but for his dedication to teaching handicapped children. The Lakeshore poolside would be be littered with crutches and canes and braces as dozens of laughing, happy, handicapped children were taught to swim. And he insisted that every swimmer be a lifesaver. "If you can't save lives in the water, you'll never swim for Lakeshore," he told his marathon students.

They trained for the long distances, swimming down the Credit River and out into the lake, ten, fifteen, twenty miles, sometimes in water as cold as 53° F. Marilyn began to win races at the CNE, one against Shirley Campbell of Fergus, Ontario, who later would try, twice, to beat Marilyn's time across the lake. In 1952, she turned professional and won $300 at the three-mile Ladies' Marathon. In 1954, there would be no women's marathon at the CNE. The big swim that year was at Atlantic City. Her teammate at Lakeshore, Cliff Lumsdon, along with Tom Park, was entering. She asked Ryder if she could try.

Marilyn's biographer, Ron McAllister, says Ryder told her: "That's 26 miles of ocean, Marilyn. You'll have to ask your Mom and Dad. It's not for me to say. I'm only your coach and trainer. The swimming is up to you." Marilyn, with her parents' blessing, decided to try. It would be her first serious test.

The Ryder team—including World Swimming Champion Cliff Lumdson and his fiancée, Joan Cooke—arrived at Atlantic City on July 1 for training and to familiarize themselves with the course around Absecon Island. By the time the race started, two weeks later, there were 39 swimmers entered and 100,000 people watching.

It was Canada's day. Tom Park won, ninety seconds ahead of Lumsdon who had been swept against pilings in the last few minutes. But way back, stroking along, sucking on pablum and corn syrup handed to her by Ryder in the boat, her body red from jellyfish stings, came tiny Marilyn Bell. She was the first woman to finish, won $1,500 and was the seventh swimmer across the line.

When the victorious Canadians arrived back at the Toronto airport, there were a few Lakeshore Club friends to greet them. Nobody for the city. Few newspaper readers knew about their triumphs. But Marilyn knew she had beaten the best and that would help in the long night on the lake, two months later.

In 1954, the CNE decided not to sponsor a marathon swimming race, but rather a single challenge by Channel swimmer Florence Chadwick in a solo crossing. There would, however, be a relay-team swim along the same route and Marilyn Bell would be a substitute swimmer. Marilyn had other plans. She figured she could take on Chadwick in a real race and she wanted to try. It was okay with Ryder, if he could raise some expense money and her parents encouraged her.

But the CNE said there would be no money in the swim for anyone but Chadwick; they had a contract with her and no one else. Marilyn Bell, they said, could swim "for the glory of Canada." At the start, however, a couple of Toronto businessmen, a jeweler who put up $1,000 and a hardware-store owner who put up $100, kicked in some prize money. Winnie Roach Leuszler decided to try, as well.

The stage was now set for one of the legendary battles between the *Star* and the *Tely*, the one against which all others would be measured. It would not be an even contest. The *Star* had more men—and women—more money and more resources in yachts, taxis and aeroplanes. And they had an airtight contract with Marilyn to be beside her all the way in the boat and for her exclusive story if she reached shore. In charge of the swim for the *Star* was veteran Buck Johnston. On the accompanying yacht, *Mona IV*, with Bell's parents and the captain, Dr. Bernard Willinsky, was reporter Mark Harrison. In the whaler *Mipepa*, with Ryder and a helmsman, was *Star* man George Bryant. The *Tely* was nowhere.

Chadwick was due to dive in at 11:00 P.M. on the night of September 6. The weather turned wet and stormy. Chadwick stayed in bed. It was nervewracking. To calm Marilyn, Bryant read her poetry. Another day passed, still raining. No move from Chadwick.

By this time, the Bell family was getting restless. *Mona IV* was turning into a party boat and Dr. Willinsky was unhappy at being away from his practice so long. Finally, the Bells' patience snapped. They would take their daughter home. They had had enough. Bryant and Harrison—"practically on our knees"—pleaded with the Bells to hang on. They agreed to for one more day.

That night, Wednesday, September 8, the weather cleared. Chadwick would go and so would Leuszler and Bell. Marilyn pulled on her black, nylon and silk bathing suit and tucked a four-leaf clover under her white bathing cap. *Star* photographer Howie Anderson drove her from the motel to the lawn in front of the coast-guard station. Ryder, waiting on the boat in the darkness, had told her earlier: "Kneel and ask the Greatest Coach and Instructor for divine guidance and strength to make this voyage, and, in our boat we will do the same."

At six minutes past eleven, Chadwick slid into the water. One minute later, rising from her knees in prayer, Marilyn walked into the lake. Seventeen minutes behind her, Leuszler began her swim—and immediately got lost. An hour later, unable to find her guide boat in the darkness, she returned to shore to start again.

But Chadwick and Marilyn Bell were on their way. It was drizzling rain but the water temperature was a comfortable 68°F and Marilyn headed out of the Niagara River and into the rolling swells of Lake Ontario. She was nearly seasick but the nausea passed. Then, horribly, an eel attached itself to her leg, sucking. She wrenched the writhing creature off and threw it away. There would be many others before the long swim was over.

At night, Marilyn had her eye on the searchlight, sweeping the sky over the Toronto waterfront as a guide. At midnight, it was established later, she passed Florence Chadwick. Now violent pains wracked Marilyn's stomach. Ryder fed her syrup and the agony slowly subsided. Bryant read more poetry.

Aboard the *Mona*, there had been trouble as well. The eighty-five-foot vessel had hit a buoy in the darkness and no one knew how much damage had been done. The passengers were shouting at the struggling girl: "Come on, Marilyn—

that's the girl. Remember the crippled children. They're cheering for you."

At dawn, vomiting and agonizingly sick, Florence Chadwick was pulled out of the water. The news encouraged Marilyn who was fourteen miles out and numb, her stomach aching.

On shore, at the *Tely* office, panic had suddenly set in. Reporters and editors, driving to work, saw the crowds piling up along the Lakeshore. By the time Marilyn Bell landed there would be 150,000 people strung out along Sunnyside Beach, the largest crowd in Toronto's history. Doug MacFarlane took over the story. In all his long newspaper life, he never had a finer few hours. And yet, years later when he was head of a journalism school, he would spend many uneasy times explaining to journalism students why he had written such a controversial page in newspaper ethics.

Reporter Ian Paterson was dispatched from the *Tely* office to hire a yacht, take a crew aboard and pick up Marilyn's route. Reporters and photographers were deployed along the lakefront. Ambulances were hired and reporter Dorothy Howarth was told to get into a nurse's uniform. MacFarlane's plan was audacious enough: the *Tely* would kidnap Marilyn Bell.

MacFarlane was something of an expert in newspaper kidnapping. He had been doing it for years, snatching sweepstake winners out from under the opposition's nose, all the way back to his days as a reporter in Chatham. Crime-story survivors — weeping mothers, mouthy lovers—regularly found themselves living in luxury at the King Edward Hotel, when they had actually intended to be at home. When they had been milked of their stories and were bewildered but sometimes delighted with the attention, they were dismissed in a taxi.

But to kidnap Marilyn Bell and keep her from the *Star* would be the absolute, goddamn end.

Out on the lake it was full daylight and fleets of boats, including three now from the *Star*, one from the *Tely* and a bunch from radio and television stations, had begun to gather around the swimmer.

Buck Johnston, who was in one of the *Star* boats, says, "One far-out memory I have of the mid-lake portion of the swim was of empty float planes drifting on the lake's surface. These were aircraft chartered by the three Toronto papers, the CBC, and whatever, to fly back film and copy to the Island Airport. While the pilots were waiting for copy and pix, they were ferried to the adjacent yachts where great parties were going on."

Marilyn was floating on her back, rubbing liniment onto her aching legs. Ryder had a blackboard and was writing encouraging messages. "The people in the boat," Marilyn said later, "kept putting up signs that great sums of money would be given to me if I finished, but I wasn't quite clear what they meant. It was an hour or two after I finished that I realized they were in thousands, not hundreds."

CNE officials, realizing they had an exploitable heroine on her way in—and Chadwick out of the water—began to raise the ante, first $1,000, then $5,000, finally $10,000. CNE manager Robert Saunders sent a pot of Exhibition ground dirt out to the *Star* boat. He wanted Marilyn to touch it.

The sixteen-year-old was now the only competitor left in the water. Leuszler, after her second start, had made it about three-quarters of the way across the lake when she had to give up and was taken out.

The *Star* and the *Tely*, now in full battle order, were exchanging headlines hour by hour. FOUR MILES TO GO, announced the *Star*. ONLY YARDS TO GO, said the *Tely*'s final edition.

But, as Mark Harrison recalled later, the *Star* editors—Borden Spears, Tommy Lytle, Jim Kingsbury—weren't caught up in the story the way the *Star* men on the spot were: "We could see the shore black with people, we knew we had a big one." Harry C. Hindmarsh, the *Star*'s crusty publisher, while agreeing to meet Marilyn's expenses, had decreed there would be no excessive exploitation of the girl by his paper. "This will be her triumph if she makes it," he told his editors. "She doesn't have to share it with anyone."

At the *Tely*, however, the editorial room was empty by mid-afternoon as every reporter, photographer, copy and off-shift editor—particularly if he was big—headed for Sunnyside. The *Star* had hired every Yellow Cab in town; these, the light cavalry of journalism, were preparing to bottle up the area where Marilyn landed. The *Tely*, however, had all the water taxis, the fast, little boats that were to prove a godsend at the end.

By 4:30, with the Toronto skyline only four miles ahead and plainly visible, Marilyn was crying. She had been in the water for eighteen hours; her head was bobbing from side to side as she tried to stay awake. The men on the *Mipepa* were bellowing at her: "C'mon, Marilyn. There's home, you've al-most made it. Keep going, keep kicking." But to Marilyn, the shoreline was a mirage that never seemed to get any closer. And there now was a new danger: dozens of boats, those hired by the papers and radio stations and many more private yachts that had come out to meet the swimmer. She was surrounded by darting craft that threatened to swamp her as she dragged along. On the *Mona IV*, her father was so angry, he stood on the prow and threw Coke bottles at the offending boats.

In the water, it appeared Marilyn was done. She was doz-ing, her legs hanging down, not moving. In the tiny whaler, Ryder looked at Joan Cooke, Lumsdon's fiancée and Marilyn's close friend, who had come out from shore to be aboard in the final miles. Cooke nodded. She slipped out of her blouse and slacks, ignoring the men in the boats around, and dived into the water. She swam over to Marilyn, laughing and shouting. Marilyn's head came up. "C'mon, Marilyn," Cooke yelled, "give them that old Atlantic City fight. You can do it. C'mon, Lakeshore girl." Marilyn looked unbelieving. Then she shook her white bathing cap with the four-leaf clover beneath. Her legs began to move. Her arms swung up and down. She was swimming again and talking to Joan and swimming. Even smiling. The boats erupted in cheers.

Mark Harrison, in the *Mona IV*, was worried. They had figured to land somewhere along the CNE waterfront where an ambulance and photographers were waiting. But he could see the dozens, now hundreds of boats ahead. And the shoreline was crowded with people. The *Tely* boats seemed to be everywhere. He radioed to the *Star* office that they had better get her away from shore as soon as she touched and over to the lifeguard station at the foot of John Street.

Aboard the *Tely* boat, Paterson heard the call on his ship-to-shore radio and immediately called MacFarlane. "Get everybody down to the lifeguard station, they're bringing her in there."

It was getting dark again as Marilyn neared the CNE break-water. Bryant was standing up in the whaler, flailing an oar. People, some of them clothed, had plunged into the water to be with Marilyn in the last few yards. One man had a hold of her swimsuit and was trying to cut off a souvenir piece. Bryant had to beat them away.

Now the two paper armies were coming together and, like all battles, the outcome would depend mostly on Lady Luck.

The Lady was sitting on the shoulders of *Tely* photographer Ted Dinsmore that day. He and reporter George MacFarlane, Doug's brother, were in a water taxi within a few yards of Marilyn as she neared the concrete wall. MacFarlane, realizing that Dinsmore needed a better shot, took a chance. He told the taxi driver to go around the end of the breakwater and inside. He and Dinsmore clambered on to the wall and ran to where the boat lights were bobbing a short distance away. Dinsmore scrambled along a ledge below the crest and wriggled between a handful of people standing on the foot-wide top.

There was Marilyn's white cap bobbing. She stretched her arm out to touch the wall. Then, suddenly, magically, she raised her head and looked straight at Dinsmore's camera. The flashbulb exploded. "I got it," Dinsmore screamed. He handed the precious slide to MacFarlane and went on shooting. There were no other photographers on the wall. He had an exclusive, the picture that everyone wanted and, somehow, the *Star* had missed.

Bryant and Ryder managed to haul the exhausted girl into the whaler. She was limp and nearly asleep but they got her up the ladder and on to *Mona IV*. The yacht steamed for the lifeguard station.

Now, the *Tely* got another break. Almost all the *Star* reporters and photographers who were not on the boats were strung along the shore at Sunnyside. And they were trapped. There were so many people and a gridlock of traffic that nothing was moving. They could see Marilyn had landed but couldn't get to the spot and, worse, couldn't re-deploy back at the lifeguard station. But there was no real panic. She was their girl, wasn't she? Weren't Bryant and Harrison right there with her? What could go wrong?

Plenty. The *Tely* had one of its ambulances at the lakeshore. The team scrambled in and told him to turn on his flashing light, fire up his siren and get the hell out of there. Head for the lifeguard station. The crowd parted, cheering, thinking that the brave, little girl was in the ambulance being carried to comfort and safety. The *Tely* men kept their heads down as the ambulance, siren screaming, bounced over curbs and around cars, the police waving them on. "My God," said reporter Ed Mahoney, who was aboard. "It was marvelous."

MacFarlane's plot began to unfold. The kidnapping was first. But he had a fall-back position—and a diabolical scheme he was keeping to himself. "Whatever happens," he told the reporters on the way to the lifeguard station, "get every scrap of conversation you can pick up, every message, every shout, every exchange between the *Star* guys. Try and get to Marilyn. Fight your way in if you have to. But get to her and get her in our ambulance. Dorothy Howarth, in her nurse's uniform will be inside. We need words, any words, that come from Marilyn, from Ryder, from her parents, anybody. Go."

The *Tely* reporters and photographers infiltrated the ranks of Yellow cabs that ringed the station, practically nose to bonnet. I noticed three ambulances, lights flashing silently, parked around the station. One was backed up right against the station door. That was ours. Howarth was crouched in the darkness inside.

As the *Mona IV* crept into the dock, Buck Johnston was stunned. Where had all those newspeople on the slip come from? The landing place was supposed to be secret. He hadn't realized the implications of Harrison's radiophone call. Johnston shouted at the police to clear the crowd away but no one moved. Johnston said Marilyn would not be brought ashore until the photographers were cleared away and all non-*Star* people hustled out. He thought it had been done. But we had slipped into crevices in the building. When the stretcher came on the slip, there was pandemonium. *Tely* men were everywhere, shouting at Marilyn and Ryder. Flashguns exploded. The stretcher went down and a reporter fell on top of Marilyn. Someone heaved him off; the stretcher handles were grabbed again and Marilyn was rushed outside. The *Tely* ambulance doors were invitingly open and Howarth in her crisp uniform beckoned the stretcher-bearers in.

Suddenly, Alexandrine Gibb, the *Star*'s top sob sister,

spotted Howarth. "Jesus Christ," she screamed, "don't put her in there. That's Dorothy Howarth of *The Telegram*." The stretcher-bearers wheeled around. Out of a barrel nearby popped a *Tely* photographer, firing away. Johnston kicked the barrel over and the photographer went down. A *Star* man raced around the front of the *Tely* ambulance, opened the door and tore out the ignition wires. That did it for MacFarlane's Plan A.

Somehow, the *Star* ambulance, now with Marilyn safely inside, scrambled out of the lifeguard-station lot and headed for the Royal York Hotel where the *Star* had booked a suite, and a doctor was waiting. The plan was to go up the freight elevator. The ambulance slipped around the back to avoid alerting the *Tely* men, who doubtless were waiting at the front by now. The freight-elevator doors opened and what appeared to Johnston to be an hotel employee was waiting. It was a *Tely* reporter who quickly began asking Marilyn questions. Johnston threw him out. By the time the elevator reached the proper floor and Marilyn was, at last, taken in to her bedroom, the *Star* crew were so jumpy they tried to throw out the hotel manager, Johnny Johnston, who was standing inside the door in tears, murmuring: "I only want to shake the hand of this brave, young lady." Marilyn smiled at him.

With the door slammed and the hotel floor sealed off, the *Tely* troops were done. They headed back for the office. They hadn't succeeded in kidnapping Marilyn. But they had the next best thing. Words. It would be up to MacFarlane to decide what to do with them.

MacFarlane called the *Tely* people together at the city desk. "Now listen," he said, "I want all of you to write every single word, gesture or sound that Marilyn or her friends or relatives said and give it to Dorothy. She has some stuff from the Atlantic City swim. She's going to write Marilyn's first-person story."

Dorothy Howarth was a slim, elegant reporter with a puckish sense of humor, a little older than some of us. She was a marvelous writer with an interesting line in scruples. On one occasion, a picture pickup, she berated me for practically blackmailing a grieving mother out of a picture of her daughter but then, a few days later, while we were combing through the rubble of a fire, Dorothy came upon a bundle of love letters from the victim to her soldier husband.

"Listen to this," she said, "wonderful, sexy stuff" and began to read me the details. I was horrified. "Dorothy, you can't use that. It's private, intimate correspondence," I said. "Like hell I can't," said Dorothy and stuffed the bundle into her purse.

But she would have no trouble with the Marilyn story. "As told to" stories were routine and this ought to be a good one. But MacFarlane had something else in mind. He knew Marilyn attended Loretto College School in Toronto and must have textbooks there. Students usually signed textbooks. So MacFarlane sent a reporter to the school to get one of her books—"some good Catholic boy to sweet talk the Sisters," as Bassett would gleefully tell it later.

He came back with some of her stuff. Inside the front cover of one book was a beautiful, almost copperplate signature—"Marilyn Bell." It was photocopied.

Now Dorothy, fed with everything we could remember, went to work while MacFarlane, with Dinsmore's incredible picture before him, began to lay out the front page. There would be only one other story on Page One—Massey-Harris was about to go on strike.

Dorothy's tale, under the massive head MARILYN'S STORY —I FELT I WAS SWIMMING FOREVER, became a classic in the tight, little world of newspapering, not only because it was beautifully and quickly done, but because on top was the photocopy of Marilyn's signature. That would engage classes in journalism ethics for decades to come.

MacFarlane, who wound up teaching such classes, had to tell them: "I had no difficulty justifying that signature at the time. But I sure as hell do now."

Although Dorothy could not be given credit for her story, everyone at the *Tely*—and the *Star*—knew she had done it. It was written in the naive, jerky style of a tired schoolgirl. Later, when George Bryant would write Marilyn's story for the *Star*, it would be professionally done, but it didn't sound like Marilyn. In later years, when Marilyn became almost a property of the *Tely*, she would tell MacFarlane: "I liked my story better in the *Tely* than my story in the *Star*."

Here it is, in part:

"I haven't got a stomach," was the first thing I said to my trainer, Gus Ryder, when they pulled me into the boat. At least that's what he says I said. I don't remember. I know I wasn't sick but I felt as if my stomach wasn't there.

I feel terrific now. All I want to do is sleep. And eat. The doctor says I've probably lost 20 pounds, not eating for—how many hours is it since I've eaten anyway? About 24? It feels like more than that.

They gave me syrup and pablum out in the lake. I think I stopped twice for syrup in the last few minutes. It's hard to remember now and it's hard to explain how I feel. They say I went to sleep twice. Maybe I did but I know I kept right on swimming.

It was the darkness and the eels that bothered me most. It was so dark that first night. I called to the boat to turn all its lights on so I could see something. They did and I felt better. But the eels kept coming around me. I could feel them. One of them fastened on my leg. I could feel its sucking mouth. It slowed me a little and finally I kicked it off.

The last two hours were the hardest. I felt like I did in Atlantic City when I swam the 26-mile marathon there—

as if I'd been swimming all my life. Every time I brought my head up I saw the same old things, the sky, the waves, and the darkness of the water again.

Even though you have boats there you seem to be alone. You can't hear anything, your mind goes blank and you just keep doing the same thing, over and over—yes, and over again.

I knew I was beginning to feel tired. It was as if I had been swimming for such a long time. At one time I didn't think I could keep going. I was so-o-o tired. Then there was a splash and Joannie was beside me. Oh my, it was great to have somebody right there beside you, matching stroke for stroke. I felt like squeezing her. Silly, wasn't it . . . ?

I didn't know about the thousands of people at the waterfront, the boats or anything else when I made the last long stretch.

Then I got the feeling I was just about there. I took a quick look and in the darkness I could make out the people's faces reflected in the light. A shiver seemed to go through me and it wasn't from the cold.

I just had to get there so I really tried to cut through the water. Then I hit the hardness of the breakwater. I think then a feeling swept through my body which I doubt I will ever experience again—I just can't explain how it was.

Howarth rather tidied up the shambles at the lifesaving station as she wound up Marilyn's girlish tale.

There seemed to be quite a few people around and a lot of flashbulbs going off. I didn't want my picture taken like that because I was sure I must be looking rather awful.

I stuck my tongue out at them and a flashbulb went off so I knew they'd caught it. I asked them not to use that one
. . .

It all seems like a dream or a nightmare. I still can't get

over the fact that so many people are interested. It seems awfully nice of them.

The men carrying the stretcher carried me along the narrow piers between the slips in the lifesaving station and I could look down over the edge into the dark water again. Don't drop me. I'm scared of water, I said . . .

It was a magnificent phoney.

At the *Star* office, Bryant, who was supposed to write the same piece, only authentic, was in real emotional difficulty. He had sweated and struggled and agonized with Marilyn through the whole ordeal. Now she was safe, sleeping exhausted in her bed. He decided he could not wake her; it would be too cruel. Her story would have to wait. But at 7:00 A.M. he decided he must begin. He woke Marilyn up, wrote a few paragraphs and sent them to the *Star*. It was the only personal story they had from their own contract swimmer.

At the *Tely*, we were gloating over Page One, Dinsmore's magnificent picture, Howarth's story under Marilyn's signature, pages and pages of pictures and stories inside. Then the *Star* arrived. We were stunned. A routine head shot of Marilyn, smiling from her stretcher. And, under Marilyn Bell's byline, three lousy paragraphs, three . . . We cheered. We shouted for Dorothy, for Dinsmore, for that cunning sonovabitch, MacFarlane. We cheered for ourselves and the *Tely*. We had beaten the mighty *Star* against impossible odds.

Bassett carolled: "We nailed 'em."

At the *Star*, recalls Harrison, "chagrin, anger, frustration."

"When the *Tely* came out," Harry Hindsmarsh, Jr., remembers, "Jim Kingsbury [the managing editor] was stomping up and down yelling 'How in hell did they get that?' George Bryant got hit pretty good."

By the second edition, the *Star* was catching up. They had the full Bell story under the too-late line: MARILYN WRITES HER OWN STORY EXCLUSIVELY FOR THE STAR. But in the professional world of newspapering, catching-up doesn't count. The readers may not know, but the peer group knows. The *Star* was humiliated, and the *Tely* sold so many papers, it nearly went broke.

The next day, Canadians had found a heroine. They wanted to see her, touch her, write to her, reward her. The gifts poured in until they filled a warehouse and the *Star* photographed Marilyn and her collie dog surrounded by them: a blue convertible, a side of beef, two live chinchillas, a budgie in a cage, vacuum cleaners and silverware and clothes and a coffee pot and a basket of apples . . . on and on. Marilyn was overwhelmed. After Atlantic City she couldn't believe Canadians cared about marathon swimming. Maybe they didn't but they cared a whole lot about guts.

And hers, the doctor said, seemed to be all right. "It's absolutely fantastic," said Dr. Frank Griffin in the *Star*, "I've never seen anything like it. After such an ordeal, you can expect a lowering of blood pressure. But hers is absolutely normal. I would say this was a surprise to the medical profession."

Toronto gave her a tickertape parade. Mayor Allan Lamport beamed: "This is one of the greatest days in the history of the city."

Marilyn got a call from Hollywood. Swimming star Esther Williams, a submarine beauty whose husband produced wet musicals, was interested in "The Marilyn Bell Story." But Esther—McAllister records—advised her not to rush into celluloid fame.

"If they want Miss Bell at sixteen," she said, "they'll want her at seventeen. Swimming Lake Ontario is one thing—and I don't mean to minimize it—but endurance, alone, doesn't necessarily make for a successful career in films, any more than winning a dance marathon means you're a menace to Fred Astaire. My hat is off to Marilyn, but I think she should finish her schooling."

So Marilyn, presumably picking up her textbooks at the *Tely*, went back to Loretto School. But the *Tely* had too good a thing to let go. Maybe they could even do an honest-to-God story next time. If Marilyn would swim for them.

And she would.

Her first marathon swim under *Tely* sponsorship—dogged by the *Star* this time—was the classic: The English Channel.

People had been plunging into that ditch and plowing across for years, ever since Captain Matthew Webb first made it in 1875. Webb used the most popular swimming stroke of the time, the breast stroke, and it took him twenty-one hours and forty-five minutes to cover the nineteen miles. Later, an Australian swimmer, Fred Cavill, watching Indians swim in South America with an overhand stroke, brought it back to Australia, added a strong leg kick and the Australian crawl was born. Almost all marathon swimmers, including Marilyn, have used it ever since.

The first woman to make the crossing under her own power was Gertrude Ederle. She conquered the gap on August 6, 1926, in fourteen hours and thirty-four minutes.

Marilyn and her *Tely* team came to Britain to train in the summer of 1955 and she finally took off from France on July 31. This time the water swarmed with *Tely* people but the *Star* coverage was a reporter named Jack Karr, a veteran of such shenanigans. He set out from France in a small boat to follow Marilyn. But, as he did not have a radio, he had acquired some carrier pigeons and had a cage full of the cooing fowl under the stern seat. The idea was to dispatch his message to the *Star* London office manager, Bill Matters, who was waiting at the pigeon roost on the Dover Coast. But when Karr got around to scribbling out his first pigeon-post story, he discovered the notepaper he had was too thick to fit into the metal container on the pigeon's leg.

What to do? Karr had an inspiration. His wallet was full of

five-pound notes, part of his vast expense account from the *Star*. Each bill was about six by four inches wide and had a generous amount of blank space. It was also very light and flimsy. So Karr scribbled out his dispatches on five-pound notes as he bobbed along to the White Cliffs. He learned later from an unhappy Matters, however, that only a few of the moneyed birds arrived, leaving Matters to fill in the gaps in the story. And Karr always wondered what had happened to the other birds with their treasured mail.

Marilyn landed at Abbotscliffe near Folkestone, fourteen hours and thirty-six minutes after leaving Cap Gris Nez, France. She was the youngest person ever to make the swim. *The Telegram* was ecstatic and sold a whole lot of papers. Bassett and the Eatons were losing money at a delightful rate.

So, undaunted, the *Tely* signed on Marilyn for the Second Great Canadian Swim in the summer of 1956—across the Strait of Juan de Fuca between the mainland and Victoria on Vancouver Island.

This time she was accompanied by two veteran *Tely* reporters and now her friends, the redoubtable Howarth and Phyllis Griffiths. Phyllis, whose gray hair mocked her incredible energy, was committed to *The Telegram* beyond all redemption. MacFarlane once mused to me that if he asked Phyllis to throw herself under a bus because it was important to the *Tely*, Griffiths would be under the wheels in a moment.

This swim, however, Marilyn Bell ran into trouble. On August 11, halfway out from Port Angeles in the snarling, tossing waves she nearly drowned. Gus Ryder and Cliff Lumsdon sent a pace swimmer, Pat Russell, in with her. But it was no good; Marilyn could not keep her head up and salt water out of her mouth. "I can't do it, Cliff," she sobbed, and the massive Lumsdon reached down into the water and hauled her out. It was heartbreaking. Her first failure. But Phyl Griffiths would not be beaten. The *Tely* immediately announced:

"Marilyn Bell will try again. She said so last night when she was pulled, limp and tired, from the icy tidal Strait of Juan de Fuca, only five and one-half miles from success. She said it again today after she woke up . . . " So, it had to be so.

And, sure enough, on August 24, less than two weeks later, Marilyn set out from Port Angeles again. And this time, as Phyl Griffiths wrote, "The Mighty Mite achieved the Mount Everest of Swims." She battled her way across the strait in 53° water and massive waves to knock twenty-nine minutes from the record of the only other person to have made the crossing —Bert Thomas of Tacoma, Washington. And she had become the first Canadian and the first woman to do it.

This time her signature in the *Tely* was preceded by the vital word "By" and Howarth had a tiny "As told to" byline beneath. But it was the same prose as her famous phoney: "Well, now I've swum the Strait, there really isn't anything else I want to do. But I'm not going to burn my swimsuit and goggles yet. Of course I want to marry. Some day. Every girl does . . . "

She did, too, a former lifeguard at Atlantic City, Joe DiLascio, and they settled down in New Jersey.

Marilyn never swam another marathon. She developed a slight curvature of the spine and became a teacher. But she has never been forgotten in Toronto. In the runup to the Winter Olympics she carried the Olympic Torch part of the way.

As tough and newsworthy as her Channel and Victoria swims were, they never approached the hysteria of the lake swim. And she set the pattern for more swim madness that was to begin—without her—the next summer.

But in the fall of 1954, Marilyn had packed up her prizes and gone home. It had begun to rain in Toronto and it never seemed to stop. Far to the south, death was brewing on the wind.

6 "The Dead Are Floating Down the River"

The police station was a grubby, cheerful place. The uniforms were usually pecking away at reports; the plainclothesmen, fedoras pulled low, toothpicks moving, read the race pages. Coffee was on.

It wasn't my territory, this west-side station. I worked the Scarborough side of the city. This was Weston, along the Humber River, a mostly blue-collar place of stockyards, stores where they sold tile, and big, hot factories where they bent iron. A lot of the people were new, from Europe since the war, and had built houses along the lovely river bottom. The rich lived high up on the river or across in Etobicoke. The Humber River, spanned by half a dozen bridges, was a wide, lazy, brown stream that began way up north of Woodbridge and flowed down to Lake Ontario. Never any trouble.

It was a warm October day but raining. I had come into the station to change film in the dark evidence closet. I had been making rain pictures—people sitting on car roofs, water in basements—not much, maybe Page Three if I was lucky. My God, it had been raining for days; the ground was full up and the water was starting to gather in pools everywhere.

The final editions of the *Star* and *Tely* had warned about a vicious storm called Hazel, moving up from Pennsylvania and bringing more rain with it. The *Tely's* last edition on Friday, October 16, carried the headline: HURRICANE "HAZEL" NEAR-ING TORONTO; the *Star* had a much smaller warning: ONLY ALLEGHENIES CAN DIVERT HAZEL, PREDICT MORE RAIN SATURDAY.

Neither paper seemed to take the storm too seriously, although the *Tely* had been on to weatherman Fred Turnbull all day. He had told them that, while he couldn't be specific, it looked as though the twenty-four-hour rainfall could be the heaviest in the city's history. He was worried the *Tely* might feature a hurricane story so, after conferring with the Forecast Division of the Malton Dominion Public Weather office, a bulletin was issued.

In the postmortems that followed the terrible weekend to come, the bulletin was much discussed:

Hurricane Hazel moved inland near Myrtle Beach, South Carolina, this morning. Highest winds are estimated at 100 miles per hour over a small area, with winds of 40 to 60 miles per hour extending 80 miles to the North and East and 40 Miles to the South and West of the centre. Hurricane Hazel is expected to continue at 35 to 40 miles per hour towards the Northwest for the next few hours, then follow a more northerly course.

The present Northerly motion of the hurricane centre is causing considerable apprehension in Southern Ontario areas. In this respect, it should be remembered that the Allegheny mountain range lies between us and the storm centre. The mountain range may break up, or materially weaken the storm's intensity, or cause it to veer off towards the Northeast. Just what effect the Allegeheny mountains will have cannot be stated at the moment, but a further bulletin will be issued at noon today.

The second bulletin, at noon, said in part that "in crossing the Allegheny mountains the hurricane will decrease in intensity with winds not expected to exceed 50 miles per hour on the open water of Lake Ontario."

The *Tely*, in addition to its main storm story, had another tiny blackface box entitled "You'd Better Take a Hold On Your Hat." It noted "the weather office said no special precautions were necessary to contend with the expected 50 mph winds except . . . hold on to your hat."

It was now eight o'clock at night and in the Weston police station cupboard it was very quiet and very dark. Suddenly, I heard the police station door slam open and a voice yelled: "The dead are floating down the river."

My God. I froze, my hand clutching the slides. This was not just a heavy rainstorm, it was death.

And, indeed, within the next four hours eighty-one people along the rivers and plains of Metro Toronto would drown and property damage would reach a total of $25 million.

When the weekend was over, Philip Murphy, who wrote the main story for the *Tely*, said in his lead: "It was the worst thing that ever happened in this part of the world, in terms of lives lost, property smashed, people homeless."

It still is the most terrible. There were awful floods—in Winnipeg before Hazel—and frightful tornadoes on the prairies and in central Ontario. But nothing matched the sheer horror of this night, neither in heroism nor in tragedy. In the years since Hazel, politicians and engineers have changed the landscape of the watershed with dams and spillways. People are no longer allowed to build houses on riverlands. But Toronto broadcaster Betty Kennedy, who interviewed hundreds of survivors for her book, *Hurricane Hazel*, says there are still certain areas—the Gatineau River near Ottawa, for instance—where people live on floodplain lands, Hazel long forgotten.

And she says climatologists suggest there is a "very definite probability" of another hurricane.

That means, according to statistical patterns, a storm like Hazel, a storm that brings more than five inches of rain within twenty-four hours, is likely to occur within thirty years. Hazel's thirtieth anniversary was in 1984.

It began with a swirl of wind in the ocean near the Caribbean island of Grenada, barely enough to flutter the skirt of a tourist lady, sniffing the nutmeg-scented air. It was October 5, 1954.

But air in motion is a dangerous thing. It is heavy—a large bathtub's worth weighs two pounds—and we live on the floor of an immense ocean of it, greater in volume than all the seas of the world.

Winds first began to be measured and scaled by Admiral Sir Francis Beaufort in 1805. He invented the Beaufort scale to help sailors in the handling of sails and rigging. A hurricane-force wind was one that exceeded seventy-two miles an hour on the Beaufort scale—"that which no canvas could withstand."

"A hurricane is a special type of windstorm, the most destructive of all," writes natural historian Frank Lane in *The Elements Rage*. "Although not so violent as a tornado, hurricanes cover a much wider area and last much longer—some cover half a million square miles and last three weeks. The total destruction is therefore greater."

Indeed, hurricanes have caused more damage in the United States than any other natural catastrophe. In the first sixty years of this century they took 17,000 American lives.

No one is quite sure how hurricanes are created. But we know they are heat engines with a warm core that sucks up water at an incredible rate. A large hurricane can slurp a quarter of a million tons of water vapor a second and carry it vast distances. In one day a large hurricane releases as much energy as a 13,000-megaton nuclear bomb.

Climatologists, studying the 800-mile course of destruction charted by Hazel from South Carolina to Canada, concluded that it was the product of "a major convulsion in the broad-scale circulation pattern"—whatever that was. In the latter stages, when she hit Toronto, some meteorologists consider Hazel was no longer a true hurricane. But she was certainly a water-carrier.

The long, slow swells that began to pound the Grenada beaches—with a slower beat, four to the minute, instead of the usual seven of regular waves—were the first sign that Hazel was born and on her way. She was the eighth storm of the year—named after a woman, as are all hurricanes—and moved so slowly at first that the "hurricane hunter" aircraft were able to track her for a record 207 hours. (A year later, two *Star* staffers, Alf Tate, a reporter, and Doug Cronk, a photographer, were to die aboard a hurricane-hunting plane that disappeared in a Caribbean hurricane called Janet.)

Then, on October 12, Hazel, now fully alive and incredibly vicious, swept north to come ashore on the southern peninsula of Haiti. It rumbled through the tumbledown towns and villages of Papa Doc Duvalier's voodoo land. In the city of Les Cayes it blew a baby right out of its mother's arms. The next day the child was found, unharmed, under a pile of wreckage. In one day, Hazel left 200 people dead—a terrible toll that drew little attention in Canada. The storm missed Florida but travelled up the Carolina coast, tearing off roofs and flattening buildings. It hit Washington, killing two people and injuring thirty-seven more, then went on through Maryland and Delaware toward New York State.

"At 11 P.M. [October 16]," wrote Kennedy, "the U.S. weather bureau felt able to take Hazel out of its hurricane class since the winds had dropped below 74 miles per hour. But Hazel was headed out over Lake Ontario towards a city that had never known even a slowing hurricane, in an area where no hurricane had a logical right to be, on a path unheard of for a tropical storm."

In Toronto, the *Tely's* managing editor was driving home from work that evening when the rain, driven practically horizontal by the fierce wind, pounded against his windshield. Doug MacFarlane turned his car around and returned to the office. He did not get home again for three days. The *Star's* Harry Hindmarsh, roused at home, ordered staff out by phone and came down to the office to stay, as well.

I left the Weston station behind the police, who were piling into cruisers and heading for the Scarlet Road bridge across the Humber River. This was a narrow, picturesque crossing, high above the water, little used now that newer bridges were complete to the south. It seemed to me the wind had died but the rain was pelting down as we drove onto the battered bridge. Below, the scene was awesome. The Humber River, normally so tame, had gone mad. It was a muddy, boiling, roaring mess. With powerful spotlights from the cruisers, we could see the turmoil of house trailers, cattle, cars, debris of every kind, sweeping under the bridge. And, as we looked more closely, bodies.

I heard a muffled scream and spun around to the other side of the bridge. It came again. The police spotlights and my exploding flashbulbs illuminated an elderly man, clinging to a branch almost in the middle of the river. His head was thrown back and he was yelling for his life. The police and newly arrived firemen ran for ropes. Then a young policeman took off his shoes and tunic. He was Richard Stock of the Toronto City Police. His fellow officers yelled at him: "Don't do it. You'll never make it. You'll drown in that torrent."

But Stock ignored them. He tied the rope around his waist

and plunged in, shouting encouragement to the old man, swimming and pulling himself along on tree branches. Suddenly the old man disappeared and, just as suddenly, Stock lost his grip. We could see him thrashing against the current, held only by the rope in the hands of his fellow officers. Slowly, they hauled him back as I fired bulb after bulb, changing slides frantically, hoping they would not all be destroyed by the rain. Stock was heaved ashore safely. The old man had disappeared. I never found out who he was.

Back on the bridge, there was no sign of a letup in the roaring river. The amount of water was unbelievable. In twenty-four hours, including the height of the storm, 7.20 inches of rain had been dumped on the city, almost double the record of 3.88 inches in twenty-four hours set in 1897. The Metro watershed had received 40 billion gallons of water from Hazel, almost 200 million tons, all trying to make its way to the lake.

By this time, reporters and photographers were being shunted all over the teeming city, from the Rouge River in the east, north to the rich, agricultural lake bed of Holland Marsh and west to the Humber.

Tely police reporter Doug Creighton was called at home, not far from the Humber where he had lived most of his life, and told the river was flooding and people drowning. "Don't be silly," said Creighton loftily, "the Humber is a quiet river. It would never do that." He hung up.

Seconds later the night editor called again: "I'd hate to fire you in the middle of a hurricane, we need men too badly, but if you don't get your ass over to the Humber right now, you're gone." Creighton went.

Toronto's rivers—Highland Creek, the Rouge, the Don, the Humber, Etobicoke Creek, the Credit River and Sixteen Mile Creek—were all in flood. And not just swirling broadly, but thundering, sweeping bridges away and tearing at their banks and bottomlands.

It was the Humber, from Woodbridge to the lake, where the surge carried death mostly awfully.

One of the loveliest spots on the Humber, where in the earlier, golden days of fall, the flame-red trees hung over the steep backs, was a section near what was called Old Mill Road, where, indeed, there was once a mill. A crew of volunteer firemen had assembled in answer to a call for help from a couple apparently trapped in their car. The eight men, led by Deputy-Chief Tiny Collins, drove their truck down to the river, where they were stopped by the white water boiling up over the road. They could see the car they were supposed to rescue and they could see there was no one in it. And then they were in trouble. Another fireman had followed them in his own car. He lost control in the water, his car hit the truck and he barely managed to clamber out and onto the firetruck before his car was swept away.

Fireman Jim Britton told Betty Kennedy later: "What were we going to do? The water was getting higher and higher. You know we grew up here. Oh, we've seen the Humber in flood. We used to go down there, little bare-assed kids. We figured, okay, fine. But the water kept coming up. Up to the tires. Getting higher. And higher . . ."

The firemen shook hands. Suddenly, the long heavy length of firehose, curled up on the truck, was whipped out by the wind and uncoiled slowly like a long white snake in the river. The truck was lighter now and unstable. Then the ground gave way and the truck rolled and the river took the men. Five were drowned.

"It was so hard to believe that they were all gone," said fireman Bryan Mitchell, who had been with the men a few hours before. "This was just like a small town. We all grew up together, ran fires together." Mitchell, who became chief of the Etobicoke Fire Department, had a fireman's axe on his office wall. It was dug from the mud where the firemen drowned.

Up in Woodbridge, the sea cadets had trucked in some whalers and were walking along beside them, in chest-deep water, getting people out of houses. At one place, a young man was on the porch with a broomstick rescuing animals floating by. He managed to save twenty-seven cats and fourteen dogs. They were loaded into a whaler without a growl or a scratch and released on higher ground. They disappeared, still in a pack.

By now, close to midnight, the streets along the rivers were jammed with hurtling vehicles—police cars, ambulances, reporters' cars, emergency vehicles of every kind. We traded information as best we could. But there was no overall picture. If this spot was bad, was it as bad as the Don or Highland Creek? Where should we be? Who the hell knows; there was chaos everywhere. I called the office and was told to try to find a street called Raymore Drive down by the Humber, south of Lawrence Avenue. There was supposed to be real trouble there. I never did find Raymore Drive. It had washed away.

It had been a short, circular street, quiet, with modest but comfortable homes. In spring, the Humber would sometimes lap up to the porches. It could cause a mess but in the summer it was lovely and in the winter there was skating right at the front door. Some people had lived there fifty years.

At about 10:30 on this wild night, the power to Raymore Drive failed. Many of the residents simply went to bed. Just up the river from Raymore was a swing bridge that people used to get to their homes. This night, as Raymore resident David Phillips started back from a date, he was astonished to see the westerly end of the bridge had broken loose and had swung out into the river with debris piling up behind it. Then the river changed course, and a tidal wave poured across Raymore Drive.

With a crumbling roar, fourteen houses along the street disappeared and, with them, thirty-six people, tumbling out of their beds, out of windows and doors, swept into the river to drown.

Fireman Mitchell watched in awed dismay. "I felt so helpless, but there was nothing anybody could do," he told the *Star* later. "The water was deep, up to our chins, and all the firemen were weighed down by clothing and boots and equipment."

The firemen tied ropes around their bodies and tried to swim out to the victims, who were clinging to wreckage and crying piteously. Their cries grew weaker and stopped.

"It was like something out of a Cecil B. De Mille movie," recalled Mitchell. "The incredible roar of the water, like the roar of Niagara Falls. It was a gigantic flood with smashed houses and uprooted trees bobbing like corks, everything going down the river so fast. Houses crashing into the sides of other houses, people everywhere screaming. And then you couldn't hear the screams anymore."

On the phone to the *Globe* was a tough and experienced reporter, Lotta Dempsey. She was sobbing.

Raymore Drive was the worst single event of the Hazel tragedy.

In Etobicoke, along the creek, firemen rescued a tiny, premature baby the *Star* featured on Page One as THE ORPHAN OF THE STORM.

The Clifford Thorpe family lived in a cottage-style bungalow near Etobicoke Creek, which was rapidly flooding. They called the fire department for help. But when a dump truck full of firemen arrived they wanted only to hand over four-month-old Nancy, along with a suitcase packed with clothes and formula. The parents and two-year-old son, Bobby, would stay. They had ridden out floods before.

The firemen took the baby, waded through chest-deep water back to the truck, only to find it had stalled. They managed to get to the roof of a cement-block house along with the child.

"The water kept climbing," fireman Norman Clift told Betty Kennedy, "until about 4 A.M. there was only a spot of roof showing. Then the spot began to get bigger and we knew the crest had been reached."

In the morning they were rescued. Down the street, the Thorpe house was gone. The Thorpes were dead.

Now, no one was absolutely sure if the baby was a Thorpe or not. The *Tely* asked if anyone could identify the orphan of the storm—"she is a bright little girl, with definitely blue eyes, large ears and she has long, thin fingers."

The child was later identified by a neighbor. And by her dog. Some days later, the Thorpe family dog appeared. He approached the baby's bed and crawled under the covers.

As reporters and photographers began to drift back to the paper, we traded stories. One of the most bizarre came from the north, the curious voyage of the house on Holland Marsh.

We learned about Harry de Peuter's adventure that night only in bits and pieces. There were plenty of houses floating down the rivers. But Harry and his family—as author Kennedy pieced together much later—were among the real Noahs of the flood.

The Holland Marsh, twenty-five miles north of Toronto, is rich agricultural land, actually the bottom of a swamp that had been drained by the local and provincial governments in 1929. The area began to be settled by mostly Dutch immigrants in 1934 and the 10,000-acre flatland became Toronto's vegetable garden. By October 1954, 3,000 people lived on and tilled the black soil, growing onions and tomatoes, celery and other vegetables. The land, of course, was very low, between foothills and drained by canals.

Charlie Davis, who farmed fifty acres in the marsh, said

later the marsh was like a wet sponge when Hazel arrived. It could not absorb any more water so it became a lake once more.

"It wasn't like down by the Humber," Charlie told the *Star*, "where there was a big rush of water. The water was really quiet and it was so dark outside you couldn't really see what was happening. But every time you looked out the door, the water had risen another six inches."

Harry de Peuter and his family had arrived a few months before Hazel, survivors of the May 1954 flood in Holland that had killed 2,500 people. They were a big family—mother, father and twelve children.

When the water started to rise, Harry nailed the front door shut, a mistake, as it turned out, because the water was now higher on the outside of the frame house. They looked out and saw a neighbor's house floating by. Then, with a jolt, their house floated off its pilings and began its voyage.

"The amazing thing was," Harry told Kennedy, "all the lights in the house stayed on, because we were moving toward the hydro lines and they were slackening.

"The house just took off like a boat, a real Noah's Ark. From 11:30 to 6:30 in the morning we floated aimlessly through the Marsh, bumping into houses, greenhouses, barns, hydro poles, everything. The area over by the Holland River had a faster current and somehow our house got caught in that and began spinning like a top, faster and faster and rocking to and fro. We all—all 14 of us—would run from one side of the house to the other when it tilted, trying to balance it out. One of the younger children actually got seasick."

The house finally came to rest in a field of carrots. They had sailed more than two miles.

In the editorial offices of the two papers, there was so much material available, it was hard to choose what to feature on Page One. The *Star* decided to go with a huge head: FEAR 30

DEAD 300 MISSING and a grab-bag of eight stories with a dramatic picture of the helicopter rescue of a couple from the roof of a house. The *Tely* used my picture of Constable Richard Stock in the Humber six columns wide and a bylined feature I wrote of the attempted rescue. The main headline said seventy-one were feared drowned—up forty-one from the *Star*'s figure—but the same 300 missing. I was ecstatic—half of Page One on the biggest news story of the year. And a color story at that.

But inside, the *Star* had some marvelous pictures, particularly a full page of some firemen forming a human chain to rescue a man who had clung to some bushes in the raging Don River for five hours. There was a whole lot more information on the front page of the *Star* than on the *Tely*'s, but the *Tely* may have had more visual impact. It was a reversal of MacFarlane's usual front-page technique. In a harangue with the *Tely*'s then city editor, Laurie McKechnie, one night MacFarlane had shouted: "The trouble with you, McKechnie, is that if you owned a shoe store, you would put one perfect pair of shoes in the window, beautifully displayed, beautifully lit. In my shoe store, the window would be filled with shoes and signs saying 'cheap, cheap, cheap.' And I'd sell a helluva lot more shoes than you."

I went to sleep on my desk. There would be more shoes to sell tomorrow.

The next morning, the rain had stopped. The wind had died. It was cool and cloudy. "Rent a helicopter," MacFarlane said. "Go up and down the Humber and get some pictures. And rescue somebody." The Bell chopper took off from the Island Airport and headed for the lower end of the river. It was an unforgettable sight. The Humber had returned to some sort of sullen quiet. But its banks were an incredible jumble of houses, trailers, cars, trees, outhouses, anything that could be ripped up and swept away. People in boats moved about the junk, looking for bodies. We hovered as firemen hauled a sodden corpse out of the mud near Raymore Drive. Farther north, at Woodbridge, a trailer camp was a mess of huge boxes, tossed one on top of the other. We kept going, looking for someone to rescue.

Finally, the pilot spotted a woman on a pebbled bit of land, beside a wrecked house, completely surrounded by water. We set down with a clatter and I got out. "We are here to rescue you, madam," I said. "The Toronto *Telegram* at your service." I prepared to photograph her climbing into the helicopter.

"No, thank you, " she said, evenly.

"Why in heaven's name not?" I asked, genuinely bewildered that she would prefer this rocky island to safety on the mainland.

"I don't like those things," she said, pointing at the chopper, its rotors spinning and clattering. "Besides, the water's going down and I can walk across in a few hours."

Damn, I thought, as we lifted away, MacFarlane's going to be mad if the *Tely* helicopter hasn't rescued someone for Monday's paper. The *Star*'s probably got squadrons of choppers ferrying people to safety in droves. In fact, above me in a light plane, the *Star*'s Buck Johnston was patrolling the same area and not rescuing anyone either. He couldn't even land.

We drifted over to Yonge Street where we could see the old iron Hogg's Hollow bridge was ripped out. The Don had torn the front lawns away from houses and they were sticking out of the newly hewn banks. At Upper Canada College helicopters were taking off and landing from the playing fields. Premier Leslie Frost had called the college principal to request permission.

He had been told by a new woman switchboard operator on his first try that if this was Premier Frost she would put him through to the department that dealt with refrigeration problems.

The Holland Marsh was a huge limpid lake whose shores were lined with banks of vegetable crates and mountains of potatoes, cabbages and tomatoes. But within a year, the marsh was pumped out again and was back to its lush productivity.

By Monday, the blood and mud were being cleaned away. A relief fund was established, kicked off by a donation of $250,000 from the *Star's* Atkinson Charitable Foundation. Reporters walked in with teams of soldiers, looking for bodies. Gail Palmer of the *Tely* reached down in the mud to pick up what she thought was a doll. It was a dead baby.

The *Tely* and the *Star* did manage to spark one curious controversy. Why, the papers wanted to know, was there no message of sympathy from the Queen? Canada House in London was credited with the comment that the palace regarded Hazel as a Grade-B tragedy. In the end, it was discovered that no one had provided the Queen with sufficient details for a message and everyone was forgiven.

In the years after the tragedy of Hurricane Hazel some good would follow. The Metropolitan Toronto and Region Conservation Authority was formed and acquired some 30,000 acres of floodplain for parks and recreation areas. Two major dams were built to control the river waters—although eleven had been originally planned. But there are still people building and living close to the placid rivers and streams in Pickering, Woodbridge and along Highway 400, which, in part, follows the Holland River north.

Craig Mather, water administrator for the Conservation Authority, told the *Star* on Hazel's thirtieth birthday that should another hurricane ever hit the area, "we won't have major devastation on our hands. We're in much better shape today."

Certainly, no hurricane called Hazel will ever kill anyone anywhere again. In the tradition of large-scale hurricane disasters, the name has been retired.

7 | The Golf Club Siege

I was asleep when the phone rang and a voice whispered: "Get out to the Scarborough Golf Club right away and wait."

"Why in Christ should I go to the Scarborough Golf Club at three o'clock in the morning?" I whispered back.

"You're on overtime," the night editor said.

"Why are we whispering?" I whispered.

"Because no one is supposed to know about this, you asshole," he shouted.

I drove out to the darkened club, along a winding, private road, and parked behind the clubhouse. There was no one there. I sat in the car, smoking and thinking about two things: the mad, mad summer and my friend, Hibby, the con man, who was going to the slammer over the trivial matter of the Mortar Mice. I was supposed to find his wife—who was walking out with a weightlifter—borrow Hibby's new baby and take her out to the Don Jail, so I could hold her up on the front lawn and he could see her before he went to Kingston for two years less a day. Now it looked as though I might be late.

This curious rendezvous had to have something to do with the swims. The madness had begun with the Marilyn Bell swim two years before and, it seemed, as soon as the ice went off the lake, greased bodies were regularly sliding in over on the American side and paddling madly for the Canadian shore, thirty-two miles away. Mind you, it had been no bad thing for those of us on the *Tely* and the *Star*, these last two summers. We were having a lot of fun. And getting rich on overtime.

The summer before, as women like Shirley Campbell, a game little girl from Fergus, Ontario; Gerda Weber, described, for some reason as "a sentimental German with thoughts of romance"; and burly Jim Edmunds had set out for fame, and a few bucks, the coverage had settled into a delightful routine. A swimmer would approach the *Tely* and ask if we would like to sponsor him/her, provide the guide cruiser and offer money for an exclusive story. Or it might be the *Star*, first. Either way, by that summer's end there had been thirty-three people in the lake at one time or another.

If we—or the *Star*—accepted a swimmer for sponsorship, or heard the other was doing so, the Admiral of the *Tely* Fleet, Ian Paterson, a capable Scot, was dispatched to load up *Miss Ginger* or *Day Dream II*, the *Telegram*'s chartered yachts, and off we'd go. The loading consisting of several cases of beer, a little hard stuff, supplies such as fried chicken or pizzas, several paperback novels and a pad of overtime claim sheets.

There we would be, sun sparkling on the water, a chicken leg in one hand, a beer in the other, lounging on the luxurious back deck of *Miss Ginger*, reading, while alongside would be some puffing, threshing swimmer, with his coach beside him, threatening to butt a cigarette in his back if he even thought of getting out. Once in a while, we'd get on the radio and dictate a progress report to the office. Or throw an empty beer bottle at the *Star* boat on the other side. It was, you know, a kind of lazy summertime.

The swimmers came in all shapes and sizes. One was a

grandmother from the States somewhere. She started out from Youngstown, New York, swimming on her back, playing a ukulele. She got only about five miles out, and I had hardly finished my first beer of the evening when she gave up and went down, the ukulele offering one final, despairing chord. I think someone rescued her.

Occasionally, as well, we would share the expenses for *Miss Ginger* with a radio station that broadcast dramatic, hourly reports on the ship's radio. And they would read a list of sponsors the swimmer had acquired. One afternoon, I was picking on pizza, while the radio guy reported on the swimmer beside us and read out the sponsors: "If this game little girl makes it," he intoned from the chest, "she'll get a service of silver from Acme Jewelers. And from Dominion Stores a year's supply of dog food. From P.J. Grample Furriers, a four-skin neckpiece . . ." I leaped to my feet, yelping: "A foreskin neckpiece, why in hell would she want a foreskin neckpiece? How many god-damn foreskins . . ."

The radio man stuttered but resumed: "I mean a four . . . skin neckpiece." His voice rose. "A neckpiece of four skins . . ." The crew and I were doubled up. God knows what the people out in radioland thought.

Regularly, a floatplane landed nearby to pick up film and deliver more beer. The pilots, of course, would join the boat parties for a while. One television crewman, stepping from the pontoon onto *Miss Ginger* with a case of beer, slipped into the water and went straight down, undecided whether to let the precious cargo go. He finally dropped it and rose to the surface, where he was roundly abused for making the wrong decision.

Sometimes we got lost out on that seamless water. There were two classic cases of geographic misfortune. During the famous Marilyn Bell swim, the *Star* lost radio contact with its boat and *Star* reporter Gerry Hall was told to get the hell out there and find Marilyn. Gerry went down to the dock and found a drunk who had a powerboat.

"Where do you wanna go?"

"I want to go out on the lake and find Marilyn Bell," Hall said.

"Okay," said the drunk, "but I don't have a compass."

Gerry had to grab a cab and race up Yonge Street to find a compass. He bought a cheap one and the boat set out.

"When I phoned from Youngstown some hours later," he said, glooming over a beer at the Press Club, "having completely missed the flotilla that was with Marilyn and having sailed right across the lake without seeing anyone, the editor, for some reason, was downright abusive."

The other occasion was the *Tely* sponsorship of Shirley Campbell, the Fergus swimmer, the year before. The *Tely*'s reporter in the outboard beside her was John McLean and her coach was a man named Max Hurley. The *Tely*'s Doug Creighton flew out in the afternoon to see what was happening. *Miss Ginger* was busy somewhere else.

"When I got there," Creighton recalled, "McLean and Hurley were practically in a fist fight. McLean had a bottle or two. He had concluded that Hurley had lost direction and was making the girl swim back to Niagara-on-the-Lake. There was no conclusive evidence as John had thrown the compass overboard."

Creighton said: "Well, I don't know but I can tell you I flew this way to get here so Toronto's over there. She'd better just keep swimming."

Campbell never did make shore and Creighton is pretty certain that she might have had she not been swimming in circles for some time.

By the following summer, the lake was awash with swimmers again, ten of them competing for a prize put up by Brading's Brewery.

By now, I had got tired of sitting in the dark car. I got out and began prowling around the building. There was light on in an office. I knocked and there was the *Tely*'s amiable assistant managing editor, Ted McCall, sipping a Scotch with the club manager.

What's up? I asked. McCall explained that Shirley Campbell, under *Tely* sponsorship, was trying the lake again. When she reached shore, she would be whipped into a *Tely* ambulance and be driven secretly to this club where I would write her exclusive story and lock her away from the *Star* for the night.

We sat for a while, nibbling on the Scotch. McCall, who was a member of the club, was telling the manager about the recent Toronto Transit Commission ferry party. Each year in the fifties, the TTC would hold this orgy aboard a ferry chugging around the harbor. Everyone got drunk. It was a marvel that no one drowned. McCall was explaining that being a newspaper executive wasn't easy. "Reporters on that ferry would get pissed, poke me in the chest and say: 'You don't know f-all about running a paper, McCall. You're just MacFarlane's flunky.'" I hoped it wasn't me. It wasn't because he added: "The next day one of them was in my office, asking for a raise. I asked him if he remembered our last conversation and he didn't. No raise."

The radio was on in the club manager's office and we were listening to reports of Campbell's progress. She was in trouble. She was swimming toward the light at the Eastern Gap of Toronto Island. But, as she said later, it never seemed to get any closer. She was beyond exhaustion and in the last half hour had been pleading with her coach, Bert Crockett: "Mr. Crockett, please, please bring the boat over." And then to her boyfriend : "Please take me out." She had been in the water nineteen hours and she couldn't swim another stroke. She was pulled out.

At the club, I stood at the window waiting for the lights to appear that would signal the arrival of the ambulance and the *Tely* team. It was still dark when they appeared. They had shaken the *Star* and, as far as we could tell, Campbell's story —of failure—was ours. But she was too exhausted to speak. Her parents insisted she be put to bed for a while. Her parents were very religious so we had brought our religion editor, Liz Cuddy, out to be with them. Liz was fiesty as hell and a good religious writer.

She went into a private room to sit with the Campbells and get their story. At one point I opened the door and heard Liz saying: "Yes, it's God's will that Shirley didn't make it. God works in mysterious ways."

"Ah yes," said the Campbells. "Our Shirley is much directed by God."

Liz saw me peering in the door, got up and came out. "I can't take much more of this shit," she said. "Have you got a drink?"

"Here's a drink," I said, shoving a whiskey into her hand. "But get back in there and tell them more about God's will, for Christ's sake. It may be all we get for the first edition."

Liz, looking more pious than ever after the Scotch, went back and closed the door.

Campbell was now firmly settled in bed. It didn't look as though anyone was going to talk to her and make any pictures before noon. The *Tely* crowd packed up its stuff and left. I was told to stay on and look after things until Campbell woke up. And to be sure the *Star* didn't get to her. What am I supposed to do if the *Star* shows up? I wanted to know. Just keep them the hell out, I was told.

I sat at the bar, feeling let down. Not only had this game lit-tle girl not made it—again—but I couldn't see any story left for me. I began to worry about getting to Hibby's baby.

146

Then, through the big lounge window, in the gradual dawn, I could see car headlights moving up the drive. One, two, three, four . . . five cars. Holy shit, the *Star* had arrived. I raced around locking doors and windows, screaming for the manager. He appeared, distress clouding his dark eyes over the rumpus. Listen, I yelled, I'll have your immigration papers cancelled if anyone gets in here this morning. He looked angry. Good.

I ran upstairs where there was a door opening to the flat, graveled roof. I picked up a handful of gravel and threw it at the cars and *Star* men milling around below. "Piss off, you guys," I yelled, "this is a private club and it's locked up for the night."

"Yeah?" someone shouted back. "Well, you listen, Sears. We know you got Shirley Campbell in there and we've got to interview her. Now let us in."

"Like hell I will," I shouted, threw more gravel and ran down to the telephone. I phoned my friends at the Scarborough cop shop and said as calmly as I could. "You guys better get out to the Scarborough Golf Club, there's going to be a riot."

"Whaddya mean, a riot?" the sergeant said. "It's six o'clock in the morning and nobody's at the club. Who's supposed to be rioting?"

"It's the *Tely* and the *Star*," I said. "For Christ's sake hurry before someone gets hurt."

"How many *Star* people are there?" he wanted to know. "I don't know, maybe a dozen or so." "How many *Tely*?" "Me," I said. "It doesn't sound like much of a riot to me," the sergeant replied.

"Listen, sergeant old buddy," I said, "I'll tell you what I'll do. You've got some people coming off shift, right? Tell them if they want a drink—all they want—to come out to the golf club. I'm opening the bar." The sergeant said he'd see if anyone on the Scarborough police force was interested in a drink at six in the morning.

By this time, the *Star* men were rattling the door handles and peering in the windows. They were making a real racket. At the top of the stairs, in the bedroom wing of the club, a military-looking man appeared in his pajamas and bathrobe, flourishing a cane.

"What in hell is going on here?" he shouted. "There's been noise all night. Now it sounds like someone is breaking in."

"There's a game little girl upstairs," I said. "She tried to swim the lake but failed a few yards from shore. Now she's exhausted. Trying to sleep. Some newspaper people are trying to break in to interview her."

"Is that so?" said the colonel. "Well, let's keep them out. You look after downstairs. I'll go out on the terrace. If anyone tries to get in, I'll cane him."

"Hooray," I said.

But I knew we were doomed unless the cops arrived. The *Star* men—and women—were big and determined. And they still had time for the early deadline.

Then, like the Seventh Cavalry, the Scarborough constabulary arrived, in plain clothes, in their own cars. There must have been two dozen of them. I let them in.

"Okay, men," I said, "the bar's open. But keep the *Star* out or it's closed again." They deployed to the bar. The manager was having a fit. "Don't worry," I said, "even if it is illegal, these are the police and the *Tely* will pay."

I phoned the office and demanded reinforcements.

The *Star* was getting in. One came up the coal shute. A cop got him and threw him out. A door banged open but the cops put down their beers long enough to hustle the protesting photographers out and slammed it shut. Upstairs, I heard a thwack and a scream. "Got one," yelled the colonel. "He was trying to climb up the balcony."

What we had here was a ridiculous alternative to war. All through the decade, in every battle, the *Star* always had more men, more money, more equipment. A good many times they won. But it was a *Tely* legend that when the brave *Tely* man stood alone, trenchcoat buttoned, a grim but devil-may-care smile on his handsome face, against an airplane-load of *Star* men and equipment, somehow virtue, decency and John Bassett triumphed.

And, of course, it helped if you took the plastic disc out of the only available telephone and slipped it in your pocket or told the local telegraph operator to file the telephone book until you were ready or maybe carried a baby shoe in your trunk to photograph at the scene of a family accident.

The Battle of the Scarborough Golf Club would go unsung because the readers really didn't notice the difference in the appearance of the two newspapers. But it helped morale to beat the *Star* as regularly as possible. As the decade wore on and the *Star* grew more and more impregnable—and won more often—there was a faint, phosphorescent glow of decay illuminating our successes. But what the hell. Drink your beer.

It was nearly noon at the club now, and Shirley Campbell was awake. The manager got her a cup of tea and I photographed her. (Later, the Canadian Tea Council phoned and said I had won $25 for my picture of an athlete drinking tea. My, my, and I never knew.)

The police went home as more *Tely* people arrived. The early deadline had passed, so we graciously let the *Star* reporters in to interview the game little girl.

I was feeling pretty good as I headed for the office, wondering how long this madness could go on. Not much longer as it turned out.

John Jaremay, a steamfitter from Toronto, became the first man to swim the lake that summer and a few weeks after Shirley's failure, Brenda Fisher got across. But one man had drowned and there was a feeling it was time to end the whole business.

There would be one more watery orgy. It turned out to be a full-scale defeat. A brewery company put up $10,000 for the winner of a mass swim on August 28. The water was freezing but some of the country's top marathon swimmers—among them Cliff Lumsdon, Tom Park and Muriel Ferguson—decided to try. Nobody made it.

The water was simply too cold, the winds too high and the waves too miserable. Cliff Lumsdon, the world champ, was hauled aboard the *Tely's Day Dream II* by "Admiral" Paterson. He was out cold. Muriel Ferguson looked as if she was dead. A front-page picture in the *Tely* showed her at the last moment, face down in the water and nearly unconscious when she was pulled in. Veteran marathoner Tom Park lasted the longest but he couldn't reach shore either. Brading's Brewery gave the three finalists $6,500 to split between them and awarded $500 each to seven others. But they gave the big prize money, $10,000, to the Canadian Olympics team going to the Olympics in Australia the following year.

It was obvious the fun was over. It doesn't seem likely that marathon swimming will ever be as popular again. It's a difficult sport to find a place to watch, other than at the beginning or the end. And it's incredibly demanding. It appears to have gone the way of marathon dancing, tiresome foolishness.

The year rolled on, full of merry pranks, merrier people.

The fifties was a money time in the big cities, fat years for most, as the postwar boom rumbled along. Bay Street was full of high-rollers, fancy women, gambling on the Stock Exchange, at the track, in the hotel suites the brokers rented by the month. And around the edges were a lot of sparrows, pecking at the crumbs, driving the big guy out to the track, fetching his booze, occasionally taking a flyer on a market tip from him. Hibby was one of the sparrows.

I had met him the year before when we were fellow passengers on a very curious train.

In 1955, the Grey Cup, for the first time, was to be held in Vancouver. And the Toronto Board of Trade thought it would be a swell idea if they chartered a train to take Argo fans across the country, carrying the Toronto message from city to city until they reached the coast. I really wanted to make the trip. It sounded like fun and it had been a long time since I had been in my home town. But I was not a sports photographer or reporter. And this was the big game. For several weeks I went to local football games with my camera, photographing the action. As Grey Cup time came close, I went to MacFarlane with my portfolio of football pictures and told him I'd like to take the fan train to Vancouver, write stories aboard and do color in Vancouver. I would also photograph the game. He looked at the pictures and said okay.

I climbed aboard the train at Union Station and made my way to the roomette with my junk. I closed the door. Then suddenly, there was the most terrible clatter in the corridor. I looked out. The coach floor was covered with lead slugs, rolling everywhere. My companion, across the hall, was holding a torn plastic bag and looking dismayed.

"The goddamn bottom fell out of my bag full of slugs," he said. "I've got to pick them up or I'll never be able to phone my wife between here and Vancouver."

He was a short, but rather bulky man, with a squashed nose

and a ready grin, the product of an open bottle of Scotch in his compartment. He said his name was Hibby and he was in business.

He was, in fact, a con man. Toronto had been getting a little hot for him lately and he decided to cool off on a trip to Vancouver. On the long trip, we saw a lot of each other, told lies, drank. I liked him and he seemed to get a kick out of knowing a newspaperman. I might be of some use someday.

The train trip was a drunken revel. But when I wrote about it for the *Tely* there was trouble. Fred Gardiner, the chairman of Metropolitan Toronto, told me I had disgraced the good people of the Board of Trade by implying there was nothing but drinking aboard the train. I was going to be thrown off. He had to speak very carefully because he was pretty far into the bag.

Gardiner wired Bassett that I was to be dumped. Bassett wired back, with a copy phoned to me: "Sears stories well received here. Image of happy group on their way to Grey Cup. But if you want your wire printed, I'd be pleased to do so as a letter to the editor."

I raised my glass to Gardiner in the club car and waved my ticket. He was pretty mad.

The *Star* covered the Grey Cup game like a blanket. Their photographers were all over the field. I knew nothing about football and seemed always to be where the play wasn't. But with the help of Canadian Press pictures, the *Tely* managed to effectively conceal the fact that their photographer was not much good. In any case, when it came to sports, the *Tely* had an ace in the hole—Ted Reeve. He could write—or rhyme or both—columns that are yellowed classics today. After him— except for Milt Dunnell of the *Star* and Bill Frayne of the *Globe*—darkness descended.

On the rollicking nights aboard the fan train going back to Toronto, Hibby talked business—the Mortar Mice Scam.

What Hibby and his pimply assistant would do, they would get in their old truck with the ladder and prowl around a rich neighborhood and every once in a while they would prop the ladder up against a house, the assistant would climb up on the roof for a while and then come down to confer. By this time, the householder, preferably a nice old lady, would be outside demanding to know what they were doing.

Hibby, concern all over his face, would walk over and say: "It's the mortar mice, good lady. They're all over the neigh-borhood. We were working down the street on a job and thought we would just check some other houses."

"Mortar mice," the lady would say, "what mortar mice?"

"Ah," said Hibby, pulling two dusty mouse corpses out of his bag and waving them in her face, "these. They were in a chimney down the street, a whole nest. They live in the crumbling mortar in chimneys and breed. Soon they're all over the house. Terrible."

The lady would frequently shriek at the dead bodies waved in front of her face and insist Hibby rid her chimney of mortar mice immediately.

"Of course," Hibby would say, "but it's expensive" and he'd name a sum to dig the little creatures out that seemed appro-priate to the lady's concern. His assistant would then scrabble around in the chimney awhile and Hibby would collect some cash, always cash.

He couldn't use the mice all the time, Hibby explained. Sometimes a sensible woman or a retired professional man came to the door. He would then explain that he had discov-ered the frams on the outlying tucks in their chimney had completely wootered and needed replacing before there was a fire in the fireplace.

"The professional men were the best for this," he said. "They didn't know what the hell I was talking about but they wouldn't lower themselves to ask for an explanation from a dumb working stiff like me. Just tell me to fix it. I really hit them."

And he had another thing going, he figured. It was that people didn't get much attention, never mind respect. He was doing a service, kind of. Like the neighborhood social worker. They would come out and talk to him on the lawn when his assistant was fixing the frams or cleaning out the mice. Sometimes it took an hour or two, if he wanted to make it look really professional and it was early in the day. He always left them feeling pretty good, if a little lighter in their big fat purses. Wasn't that worth something?

Unhappily, what Hibby was doing was either fraud or very close to it and the fraud squad in various towns, upon receiving complaints from some member of the family who realized Mother had been had, blew the whistle and Hibby had to flee.

But this trip had been financed with a real interesting score, he said.

He had been in North Bay the week before, dropping around to houses with his mortar mice, when he came upon a couple of old ladies who were really friendly and asked him in for tea to discuss repairs.

On the wall of their living room, Hibby noticed a whole series of war savings certificates in various denominations— $100, $200, $500—all framed. "Oh yes," one of the women said, when he inquired about them, "during the war we sent money to the government as our way of helping and they sent us these scroll things. We had them framed. But we're tired of them now and we're going to take them down. Would you like them?"

"Oh no," said Hibby, licking his chops. "I couldn't really, although they are very pretty."

"We insist, don't we, Nell? Now when you get finished with

the chimney, come in for your money and you can have the pictures."

Hibby got back to the hotel with an armload of war bonds, which he promptly cashed. The phone rang. It was the fraud squad.

"Listen, Hibby, you snatched those certificates from those old ladies. Their brother called. You're in trouble. Get down here."

"Oh, no," said Hibby, "they were a gift. You phone and ask them."

The ladies wouldn't budge. They had given the certificates to that nice man, Mr. Hibbert. Now you leave him alone.

Hibby left town, snatched a suitcase and his bag of slugs, kissed his wife goodbye and caught the Grey Cup train.

I didn't see him for a while after I got back because the *Star* seemed to be kicking our ass regularly and MacFarlane was getting real broody. One day, they had a story from up north about a Jehovah's Witness preacher who had advised one of his flock not to accept blood after an accident and she had died.

"Get up there and interview that preacher and find out how it feels to play God," MacFarlane said.

I had a helluva time finding his shack, buried way in the bush, north of North Bay. I knocked on the door and was told to go away. How could I go away? I had driven 300 miles to get here. I had to have an interview. I begged, I pleaded, I swore that I'd be fired. Nothing. The door remained shut. Finally, I shouted: "Sir, if Christ had died on the Cross and there had been no one there to bear witness, no reporters as it were, who would have known about His sacrifice? Where would Christianity be today?"

My voice soared. My heart pounded. The door opened.

"Come in, my son," the tall man said. "We'd better talk." We talked for an hour. I photographed him with a Bible in his hand. Good stuff. I was saved.

On the way back, the office said I was to stop in at Owen Sound. The *Star* had found a woman's skeleton in the bush. It looked like murder. The woman had been missing since summer.

When I got there it was snowing like the devil. The police were trying to search the area where the body was found but there was too much snow. There was supposed to be some jewelry. And they wanted a weapon. The *Star* had gone. The story was dead. I was cold.

Then it occurred to me what was really needed here were flamethrowers to burn the snow away and clear the search area. The army was not far away at Barrie. I called the office, got our army expert, Herb Biggs, on the phone and suggested he dig up some flamethrowers. And, goddamn, if the army didn't agree to help. Our afternoon edition carried a big story about flamethrowers on the murder scene. The *Star* had to send their reporters back.

The police were furious. What the hell could they do with flamethrowers? Any evidence would be burned to a crisp. The army had already figured that out and in an hour or so a whole convoy of army trucks showed up—with tent heaters. Tent heaters? What kind of picture would that make, a bunch of canvas funnels snaking around the ground? But it did work. The snow was cleared in the immediate area, jewelry and a knife found nearby. I set out for Toronto again. I passed the *Star* car on the way out. "Where the hell are the flamethrowers?" they wanted to know. "Just keep going. And get some matches. The flamethrowers need a light."

Over the next year I saw Hibby quite a bit. Every time he would score, he'd show up at our place, swinging a bottle of Chivas, flashing a roll and carrying huge stuffed toys for the kids. My wife, Meg, didn't think much of him. He was, after all, a crook who defrauded old ladies. He was foul-mouthed and frequently pissed. I liked him.

And he often had good stories for me—about the guy with the newspaper box on Jarvis Street who rented guns for robberies or the politician who had to flee the fire in the cathouse. He hung around Bay Street a lot, doing this and that. Once, at noon, he took me through this shabby old office building not far from the Stock Exchange. When we got off the elevator, we were in some kind of Arabian Nights living room, gorgeously bad taste with red cushions, purple drapes, glass tables, the lot. "Hi, Frank," Hibby said, "I brought a friend for lunch." They tore the place down one day and built a bank.

Hibby disappeared for a week one time and when I asked him where he'd been, he said he'd been doing a favor for a friend—collecting for the Mother Cabrini Fund. Mother Cabrini was a New Yorker and a candidate for sainthood. Hibby had been touring the whorehouses in upstate New York collecting money to assist her campaign for elevation.

"I'll tell you," Hibby said, "those whores are real generous."

But now he was in trouble. He had phoned and said the cops were after him for something a couple of guys from Buffalo had done. Get a lawyer and give yourself up, I said, there's nothing I can do.

It was an interesting scam as he explained it in the Radio Artists Club before going to the station.

The two guys would find a mooch with money in the bank. Then, posing as security men from the bank with some kind of hoked-up identification, they would call on the mooch and explain they were after a crook who had been defrauding the branch. They wanted his cooperation briefly. He was to write a check as bait for the guy; they would take it to the bank and deposit it in the crook's name. He would know he hadn't that much money in his account and if he tried to withdraw it they would have him. Shit, I said to Hibby, who would buy that? You'd be surprised, he said.

Anyway, after they got the check, a third man, posing as a telephone repairman, would call on the mooch and ask to test his extension upstairs. There was trouble in the neighborhood. His fellow cons, with careful timing, would approach the bank manager to cash the check and insist he call the mooch to confirm it was all right. The manager would call, the fake repairman would answer, give his okay, and away they'd go, pockets full.

The cops figured Hibby was in on it somehow. They wanted him for the mortar mice anyway. He told me he had nothing to do with the Buffalo guys. Maybe he didn't. But he was convicted and given two years in Kingston Penitentiary.

He said he could do it standing on his head but he would like to see his baby before he went. So Meg and I located the wife, borrowed the baby and there we were, standing on the lawn of the Don Jail, swinging the kid, while Hibby waved from behind bars. Very touching.

After he got out, Hibby made a pretty good living selling towels to whorehouses in Toronto. And some to me at a cut rate. But he was getting old. I helped him get a senior citizens' apartment over a bar downtown. "The old pelicans in the place don't like me partying," he said. "But they die like mice in that place so they won't complain long."

Today Hibby lives, still above a bar, on a beach in a tropical country. I don't know how. He sends me a dirty postcard now and then and suggests I visit. Maybe I will.

It had been some year, 1956. The *Tely* circulation peaked at 270,000 and the paper was at its height. Some of the best stories were carried in a little brass tube that ran under Bay Street from the court house.

8 | When Lawyers Were Heroes

Dave Humphrey was sitting in the death cell with his client, who was due to be hanged early in the morning, and Dave was telling him he was pretty lucky.

Robert Fitton, who had strangled a little girl with her own green scarf and thrown her in a snowbank so the tears froze on her face, was looking a bit skeptical. Who the hell was Humphrey, the big shot lawyer who had failed him, to call him lucky?

"Well, look at it this way, Bob," said Humphrey, clearing his throat, "you know the hour and the day you're going to die and you have prepared yourself for God. You know that Jesus didn't come to earth to save the Eatons and the Simpsons but to save sinners like yourself. Now, if you've truly repented and made peace with God, you're lucky because you'll be in heaven tonight.

"Now, you take me, if I was hit by a car tonight and was killed without having prepared myself, I'd be the loser and you'd be the winner."

That Humphrey, in the fifties, was a young smoothie. Jack

Batten, who chronicled the adventures of a lot of Canadian lawyers, many of them from the great criminal decades right after the war, says Humphrey was the Great Entertainer of the criminal-defense bar.

"And he looks the part," wrote Batten, "a husky man with a broad expressive face and eyes that can nail a witness or an audience at thirty paces. With his sharp suits and his reper-toire of gestures that underline punchlines, he's the sort of natural comedian—an upbeat Rodney Dangerfield—who could work one of the high-roller rooms on the Strip at Vegas."

Criminal lawyers were heroes to the papers in the fifties. Every reporter knew the names and the reputations of the great ones—John Robinette, Arthur Maloney, Arthur Martin, Joe Sedgwick, Charlie Dubin, Dave Humphrey.

Some of them—Maloney, Dubin and Humphrey—were big shooters, rich, flamboyant, always ready with a drink or a quip for the grubby, admiring circle of court hacks. Some were austere—Robinette, Sedgwick—at ease among their peers at the Advocates Club but distant with the press, mandarins of the law.

Court cases, when these men were involved, were news, and reporters turned out thousands of words of running copy as a poor maiden described how, after all she had done, her affections were alienated and she thought maybe a hundred thou would make it right.

Or when Arthur Maloney, with a kind of casual insouci-ance, would tell the bench in a rape case, where the offense took place on a driveway newly laid with gravel, that his defense would be consent.

Or the look, by God the haughty, unruffled look, on Arthur Martin's face when things looked black for his client. Such as the time when he was defending a Hamilton man on a murder charge and the court was told by a lady who was there that Arthur's client had killed a child and brought the body to her home, encased in cement. When the court rustled, Arthur looked about calmly as though wondering, "What's all the commotion about?"

The three Toronto papers—the *Tely*, the *Star* and the *Globe*—managed a joint police and court bureau in the fifties, with reporters filing the same story, in routine cases, to all three. Stories would then be rewritten on the desk. The court bureau was run by a dreary, pompous little man, Bert Kemp, whom the *Tely* had once engineered into the office of mayor. Copy was sent through a pneumatic tube that ran down Bay Street and branched off to the appropriate offices.

But the real reporting work and the good times came at places like the Metropole Hotel on King Street in whose dusky tavern Arthur Maloney would hold court, night after night, for an audience of newspapermen, young lawyers, cops, taxi drivers and hangers-on who were not welcome at the Albany Club.

Or at the Chinese restaurants, not far from the courts, where a tumbler of Scotch and some garlic ribs could be put on the expense account.

"In those days," Humphrey recalls, "the criminal bar was a small and identifiable bar. It was before legal aid. There weren't all that many court cases. So, those who were in the criminal bar were well known. When I started, in 1950, there would be maybe fifteen lawyers, more or less, who did criminal work full time and another ten or fifteen who dabbled. Today, there are a thousand lawyers who think they're criminal lawyers. Everybody's entitled to a lawyer now. It was more fun then. Everybody tended to be more of a character— judges, crown attorneys, defense lawyers . . . Now everybody has to behave themselves, work a lot harder, nothing is funny.

All sincere, hard-working people. One-third of our cases were for nothing in the fifties."

The Fitton case was one of them.

On the night of January 18, 1956, Linda Lampkin, who had just turned thirteen, left her dancing class in downtown Toronto and set out for her home in York Township. Later that night, her body was found—she had been strangled and raped, in that order—by a fuel-truck driver in a snowbank among the oil storage tanks on Toronto's east-end waterfront. A red mail truck was seen in the vicinity at the time and, later that night, police confronted Robert Fitton, the truck driver, with a murder charge. He fainted.

The *Tely*'s night police reporter, Bert Petlock, quickly rounded up Fitton's wife and family, spirited them down to the King Edward Hotel to keep them from the *Star*, and began to interview them. They were willing but figured Bobby might need a lawyer, what with one thing and another. Did their new friend, Bert, know a good one? Of course, said Bert and phoned Dave Humphrey.

On the evening Fitton was to be hanged, nearly a year, a trial and an appeal later, Humphrey came to the Mandarin Gardens restaurant after informing Fitton in his death cell about his good luck.

It was a very tough night. He couldn't help talking to a bunch of the boys about what a criminal lawyer should never talk about: Where had the defense gone wrong and could he have done it any differently?

"I flirted with the idea of Linda as a tease," he said. "She certainly looked older than thirteen. But I had nowhere to go and whatever sympathy I might have had for a young man who might hang would have gone right out the window if I started accusing her of something I couldn't prove."

But then Humphrey told a strange and disturbing tale.

"There was a fellow called Paul Caccia," he said, chewing on a rib, "whom I prosecuted once for robbing a gas station. A fellow from the *Globe*, Fred Thompson, took up his case. He got Arthur Martin and there was a new trial. He was convicted again. Thompson was a vicious man with a tendency to rape people.

"And he was, by coincidence, Robert Fitton's brother-in-law.

"One day, during Fitton's trial, Bob called me in and said he was going to tell me the truth. He hadn't strangled Linda. It was his brother-in-law, Paul Caccia, who had done it. Caccia was riding in the mail truck, Fitton told me, when they had picked up Linda. He said Caccia had got in the back with the girl. He heard some sounds. Caccia tapped him on the shoulder and said, 'Hey, she's dead.' The two of them dropped the body off on Commissioners Street. And Fitton said Caccia told him if he told anybody about the murder, he and his wife were dead.

"That was Fitton's story," Humphrey said. "If I believed it, it would only make Fitton an accessory after the fact. I would call Caccia to court, have Fitton testify and Caccia would go nuts. It would have a pretty dramatic effect, maybe even got Fitton an acquittal.

"But one doesn't lightly accuse a man of murder. I leaned on Fitton pretty heavily, told him I was going to give him a lie-detector test and a professional could tell if he was lying. If what he said was not true I was dropping the case.

"Fitton said, 'Okay, Mr. Humphrey, it's not true.'

"But here's the thing. Supposing I had not pushed Fitton so hard. Was it my duty to threaten him in that way? Ethically, I could have said, thank you, this is the key to our case. If, under penalty of perjury, you are prepared to say it was Caccia and not you, then go with it.

"If he had, he might not be hanging in the morning. I don't know."

Humphrey, now a judge, still thinks about the Fitton case from time to time. And so many others his friends remind him of. Like the football player he defended for rape. His defense was consent because, among other things, the linebacker's relationship with the airline stewardess was lustful. Once, on a short cruise, they had kept score of the number of times they had had sexual intercourse. The tab, pinned on the door, had reached fifty-five times before they returned to port. Humphrey's client got off. As a victory gift, Humphrey gave him the tie he had worn in court. It had little pigs all over it and the initials "MCP" for Male Chauvinist Pig.

There was another reason why Humphrey's friends from the fifties link him with football. On a memorable occasion at the 1957 Grey Cup game between the Hamilton Tigercats and the Winnipeg Blue Bombers at Varsity Stadium in Toronto, Humphrey and some friends were sitting right on the sidelines. A Hamilton defensive back with the rhythmic name of Bibbles Bawel intercepted a pass and was heading for daylight. But as he scurried down the sideline, Humphrey stuck out his foot and down went Bibbles, ass over teakettle. Humphrey snuck away in the crowd and it was weeks before he confessed.

Thinking about the fifties crooks from his current perspective from the other side of the bench, Humphrey concludes, "They don't seem as professional as they once were. In the fifties, they all had their specialties—robbers, safecrackers, pickpockets, mortar mice. They all wore their hair short, came to court on time, nicely dressed. They called the officers sir, and pleaded guilty like men if they had no chance."

While the reputations of the great criminal lawyers certainly matured in that remarkable decade, many of them had been ripening since the war. The man who was to become the dean of Canadian lawyers and perhaps the most gifted courtroom advocate in the history of the Canadian bar, leaped into press prominence at a trial before the decade opened. It was the Evelyn Dick case, the most bizarre, most talked-about, most heavily covered criminal trial of the postwar period and it made John Josiah Robinette a celebrity.

Travellers arriving in Toronto—as I did—in the early fifties were not long in town before they were treated to the comic utterance that grew out of the Dick murder: "You cut off his arms, you cut off his legs, you cut off his head. How could you, Missus Dick?"

And, indeed, Evelyn Dick, a sweet and generous Hamilton lady, had been convicted of murdering and cutting up her husband, John Dick, a driver for the Hamilton Street Railway, whom she had left on their wedding night. Evelyn was a Steeltown courtesan, carefully trained by her mother to please men. And that she certainly did. At her trial she estimated she had slept with 150 men before she was 25, one, to the surprise of the bench, the trial judge's son. "I never knew a woman so anxious to please," one of her lawyers said.

During a brief interval, when the sheets were cooling, she married Mr. Dick but fled back to her mother's bed on the wedding night after an argument with her new and baffled husband. On the night of March 16, 1946, a bunch of kids came upon a singularly gruesome sight in the wooded area on Hamilton Mountain—a male torso minus arms, legs and head. It turned out to be the unfortunate Mr. Dick, last seen in one piece ten days earlier.

Evelyn was arrested after blood was found on the steering wheel of a car she had borrowed that day; fragments of bone and teeth were found among the furnace ashes in the basement of the house she shared with her mother and more human ash in the ruts of the alley outside. At the home of her

father, Donald MacLean, police found an axe, saw and butcher knife, a pair of black shoes flecked with blood and a .32-
caliber revolver, recently fired, of the sort that had done in
Dick. A baby, encased in cement, was also discovered in a
suitcase in the attic. Murder charges were laid against Evelyn;
her lover, Bill Bohozuk; and her parents, the MacLeans.

Evelyn told a variety of stories, most of them centering
around the "Romanelli gang," who, she said, had shot and
killed her husband. Police cautioned her at various times and
places but not in every circumstance—an oversight that
would cost the crown dearly.

The case was a sensation with the Toronto reporters—and
many from the United States—crowding into the Barton
Street jail to try to talk to the lovely Evelyn. She was shower-
ed with gifts on her twenty-sixth birthday, celebrated in her
cell. And each morning during the trial, her guard smilingly
presented her with a piece of his wife's homemade cake. The
courtesan would blow him a kiss.

Evelyn was convicted. She, somehow, had heard of a rising
young attorney, John Robinette, and asked him to handle her
appeal. Robinette agreed, believing the crown had a weak
case and the judge's charge to the jury was flawed.

Robinette was an imposing six-footer, running to plump—
he had been called "Fats" as a boy—who had led his class at
Osgoode Hall. During the depression he had taught at Osgoode and before the Dick case had handled only one murder
in which his client had escaped the noose on grounds of
insanity.

But in three days of carefully constructed argument he won
a new trial for Evelyn on the grounds of improper cautions by
the police and errors in the judge's charge. The world press,
titillated by the sexy circumstances, descended on Hamilton.
The *Star* and the *Tely* ran page after page of testimony at the

new trial. Suddenly, everyone knew who John Robinette was. "The trial court is the greatest theater in the world," a judge later said, praising Robinette's performance as an actor. He persuaded the jury that there was no way to connect the demure Evelyn with the actual killing and she was acquitted. Her mother had earlier been dismissed for lack of evidence, Bohozuk was found not guilty and her father went to jail for five years—not for murder, the charge was withdrawn, but for stealing streetcar tickets.

But there was still the baby in cement. "There was a definite feeling that Mrs. Dick had to pay some kind of penalty for the sort of life she led," Robinette said later. "The court was determined to punish her, so was the jury. . . ."

Evelyn got the maximum for the baby killing, a life sentence. But no one was ever convicted of killing and cutting up poor Mr. Dick. Evelyn served eleven years in Kingston, learning French and dressmaking. She played an angel in a Christmas pantomime. After being paroled in 1958, she went to live, anonymously, in a southwestern Ontario town.

Robinette went on to save sixteen other clients from the gallows, losing only one—cop-killer Steven Suchan.

Another Toronto lawyer, a fifties star, began his ascent defending a client in the Dick case. Arthur Martin got the lumbering Bill Bohozuk acquitted of killing babies and carving up Mr. Dick. In fact, in his long career, Martin won 90 percent of his cases, many of them handed to him by other lawyers who thought they were hopeless.

Martin was thirty-nine in 1953, a burly, heavy-jowled man who went out of his way to avoid reporters. It was a deliberate technique, he once explained. He didn't want juries to see a famous lawyer called into the case to get a client off. He wanted them to see an unknown man, fighting for another's life.

Covering one of Martin's cases was not only fascinating for

reporters but for other lawyers as well. Young counsel would fill the court benches to watch him. He never seemed to be fighting vigorously, preferring to sit at the table—which never had paper or law books on it—hands folded, looking calm and confident. He would never shout, in today's television style: "I object. . . ." but rather, rise slowly and say softly: "Please . . ."

One of Martin's students used to say that Martin never picked his cases: "he operates just like a cabbie, taking on all fares."

But he had one invariable rule: "I will defend anyone only once." He did not want to become an underworld mouth-piece. He would not take civil cases, some worth millions of dollars, preferring, instead, to deal solely with criminal law. Charlie Dubin, who was one of Martin's students and went on to become a distinguished counsel and the *Tely*'s lawyer, once had a very big civil case and succeeded in persuading Martin to help him. They met for a few sessions but Martin couldn't take the work seriously and asked that Dubin release him from his obligation.

"It all seemed a silly puzzle to him," Dubin said later. "He couldn't care less how the fight over the money came out. At the time, I know he was quite worried about a carpenter who was in danger of going to jail for forty days."

Martin's dedication to the law was prodigious. A bachelor, his home was mainly in his office where he worked day and night. He never took a vacation, except a weekend or so at summer recess. And he never owned a car, preferring the qui-et time to think about a case in a taxi.

"Fighting the crown every inch of the way, a lawyer is not only protecting his client," he would say, "but upholding a great principle of justice—still not enjoyed by over half the world's people—and thereby protecting the liberty of all free men."

Another fifties lawyer, a man who went on to be a distinguished parliamentarian, enemy of capital punishment and provincial ombudsman, was much more of a swashbuckler. Arthur Maloney, an Irishman from the Ottawa valley Maloneys, was every reporter's favorite lawyer. He bought the most drinks, gave the best parties, knew the most interesting crooks and could always be found at the Metropole and tapped for a quote.

He defended 125 murderers in his career and God knows how many rapes, burglaries, hit-and-runs, assaults and other mischiefs. One story, he told writer Pat Conlon, was his first rape case, the one on the gravel. The judge was giving the young lawyer such a hard time that Maloney, unthinking, lit up a cigarette. "I did it unconsciously," he said. "I was unaware of what I was doing, because I'd been so unnerved by the judge." There was a loud yell from the bench: "How dare you smoke in my courtroom?" Maloney butted out, apologized and composed himself for defeat.

The jury returned and announced: "Not guilty." Now it's an offense to query the jury about its verdict, but it was okay then and Maloney confessed to the foreman he was surprised by the verdict. The foreman said: "You did just fine, young fellow, just fine. We weren't going to let that bastard the judge push you around."

In the fifties, his technique finely honed, it was a pleasure to report a Maloney case, particularly if he was demolishing a specialist witness:

"Now, would you agree with that statement, doctor?"

"Certainly not."

"Well, do you know what I'm quoting from?"

"No."

"It is your own distinguished work on bloodstain technology, doctor. Your own words . . ."

"But, that was in 1917 . . ."

"No more questions, your honor."

Maloney was from Eganville, eighty miles down the valley from Ottawa, the youngest of eleven children, and their home spawned a legion of priests, nuns, doctors and lawyers. Maloney was a hard drinker and heavy smoker, knocking off the Scotch from time to time but always ready to pour one for somebody else. He was always nicely turned-out in yesterday's suit and a twisted, sardonic smile, the result of a slight harelip.

Dave Humphrey says Maloney was a model advocate. "He always argued with enormous fairness and honor. He used to convey a natural sympathy for the accused and it wasn't long before the jury shared that sympathy. I've seen him argue some very unpopular cases and emerge with the respect of everyone."

Maloney lost only one client to the hangman, Leonard Jackson, who was in on the killing of policeman Eddie Tong. It deeply depressed him. "I couldn't help thinking that if their lives had been spared they would have been great influences for good in the prison. Jackson's last words to me were, 'You've been my lawyer on earth and I'll be your lawyer in heaven.'"

When he was elected to parliament, Maloney delivered eloquent speeches against capital punishment. But, perhaps his most memorable political moment was when John Diefenbaker, harried and on the verge of humiliation by his own party, walked into a party meeting and virtually everyone remained seated and mute.

Maloney, who did not greatly like Diefenbaker's style of leadership but admired his guts and his contributions to parliament, rose slowly to his feet and said, "When John Diefenbaker walks into a room, Arthur Maloney stands up."

Maloney, in his fifties trial days, used to think that trials were an uneven contest. As he told Conlon, it was the little guy versus the big, big guy.

"The vast apparatus of the state is something I've always referred to in addresses to juries because the prosecutor has on his side trained investigators, blood analysts and experts in every conceivable field of science. And these all combine to give the prosecutor a prepared brief which he is then able to present against the accused person. The accused is in a totally different position. Invariably, he's poor by comparison, no matter how much money he has. He couldn't possibly afford the cost of all those important aids to his defense that are available to the prosecution.

"In this unequal contest, the great machine of the state comes to a halt when it comes to the jury. The jury is the buffer between the state and the individual."

On the *Tely*, when a reporter got in trouble—or for that matter, the publisher—Charlie Dubin was the man to call. He handled libel.

John Robinette—as the lawyer for the Canadian Press and the Canadian Daily Newspaper Publishers Association—was the premier newspaper lawyer and his advice was clear enough: "The basic rule is to make certain the newspapers give equal prominence to the other side."

Publishers don't like libel cases and not only because they might be expensive. It can be embarrassing if, day after day, the paper has to report some singular stupidity.

One libel case against the *Tely* that Dubin won was curiously handled. It seemed we had written a story about a "thief" who robbed a drycleaners but was identified by the ticket he left for his newly cleaned pants. Despite the fact he had simulated a gun and threatened the clerk, he was acquitted.

We were in trouble because we had said "the thief left his cleaning ticket." When it turned out he was not a thief, he got a lawyer and sued.

I was instructed to cover the trial and write a lengthy news story each day. But the story never went farther than the publisher's desk. Bassett wanted to know what was going on, but to hell with readers. It felt very strange to have a readership of one—and especially that one.

The trick in covering court stories in the fifties was learning to do running copy. Both the *Star* and the *Tely* had experts, and it was a considerable skill. Few knew shorthand until the Brits arrived in the middle fifties and, trained in speedwriting on Fleet Street or as cadets in Australia, they swept the profession. For the rest of us, it was necessary to scribble one key word in each sentence and trust our memory when we reached a telephone. Or, even more difficult, to write the story clearly and legibly as it unfolded in court to be transmitted down the Bay Street tube. It was not unusual for the *Star* and the *Tely* to devote one or two full newspages to the running copy of a spectacular trial.

Some reporters became experts in the law. One veteran court writer was even appointed to the bench. But he lost his job when he sympathetically agreed to drive Mrs. Edwin Boyd to Kingston Penitentiary to visit her bank-robber husband. He wound up in a motel with the distressed lady, someone blew the whistle and he promptly died of a heart attack.

The jousting between the great criminal lawyers of the decade was not always about violence and death. Sometimes it was about politics and greed.

Walking down Bay Street on a spring day in 1955 I was stopped by an acquaintance involved in the politics of Scarborough, my booming beat. "Do you know," he asked, "where Crockford got his Cadillac?"

"No," I said, thinking that Reeve Oliver Crockford of Scarborough probably had made enough wheeling and dealing in Scarborough to have one delivered.

"He got it from a developer," the man said.

Now here was a hi-de-ho. In Scarborough, developers were gods. But they must not bestow gifts on municipal politicians, at least not gifts as big and expensive as Cadillacs. That sort of thing could look bad.

The Bay Street man gave me the name of the dealer where the car had been purchased. Back at the office, I asked a reporter who was going up that way to see what he could find out. He called back shortly, a bit excited. "It's the damnedest thing," he said. "The car was paid for by Walter Pugh of Dorset Park Developments. But the salesman makes kind of a hobby of listing famous people who buy Caddies and he's shown me a book that lists Crockford as the owner."

"My, my," I said, "there's a lot of sin in the world. See if you can photograph the book with Crockford's name and away we go."

The story built slowly but it built. And the *Star*, by coincidence, had come upon another bit of mischief involving four checks for $500 each sent to Scarborough Township officials and council members. That was altogether too much, even for freebooting Scarborough, the fastest-growing township in the land. There had to be an inquiry.

And the man chosen to act as counsel for the commission —in effect, the prosecutor—would be Joseph Sedgwick.

Joe Sedgwick was another fifties legend. Morley Callaghan worked for him once as a law student, until Callaghan sold his first book. In the early thirties, Sedgwick had prosecuted Communist leader Tim Buck. And three years later, he hit it big with the Case of the Kidnapped Tycoon. He prosecuted a Cincinnati bookmaker who was charged with kidnapping

Ontario brewery baron John Labatt and holding him for $150,000 ransom. Labatt was kept chained and was shaved daily by the kidnappers who set him free in Toronto after the ransom was paid. He identified the Cincinnati bookmaker, David Meisner, as one of the kidnappers.

Sedgwick did such a good job as prosecutor that Meisner was sentenced to fifteen years in prison, even though he was innocent. He was released and exonerated later when another man confessed.

After the war, Sedgwick defended one of the Gouzenko atom spies and won an acquittal. He was fifty-seven when he was called to Scarborough, portly, hair going white, a genial fellow much given to gossip and anecdote but merciless in court.

His weight was a matter of some speculation by the local hangman, Jack Ellis. Ellis walked into Sedgwick's office one day with a rope he had used in his last $100 job. He was taking it to the chief coroner, who collected such souvenirs. And he was explaining to Sedgwick about the "stands," the number of windings above the loop, and the length of the drop.

With an eye on Sedgwick's stout figure and short, thick neck, the lawyer would tell his pals later, John Ellis said: "Now for you, Mr. Sedgwick, I'd have about four stands and a short drop."

He seemed to think rape was pretty funny and told a woman reporter once about the flat-chested girl who had tattooed on her tummy: "In case of rape, this side up."

The judge who would conduct the bribery inquiry was Robert Forsyth, and Crockford's lawyer was Arthur Maloney.

Crockford was a little fellow, bantam-tough, who had publicized Scarborough, its "Golden Mile" of factories, its hundreds of acres of development from farmyard to ticky-tacky houses, its growing municipal wealth, up and down the land. But it had not been a good year for him politically so far; he had lost a run for the provincial legislature. And things were going to get worse.

But Crockford knew who was out to get him, besides the papers. It was "mud slingers, scum and left-wingers" who were creating scandal over "small potatoes."

"Subdividers have done a wonderful job in Scarborough," he told the *Star*. "Nobody has to pay for anything. If their cause is right and just they get what they want."

During the inquiry, Crockford said he had, in fact, paid developer Pugh for the Caddie in three payments, in cash, without receipts. There was a lot of cash moving about in the township in those days. The inquiry was told of one deal in which Crockford received $7,000 in bills.

When Crockford was paying off Pugh, he said he gave him $2,000 in cash.

Sedgwick asked the reeve if he carried that kind of dough around with him regularly. Crockford allowed as how he sometimes did. "That would be a pretty big bundle," Sedgwick said, pulling a cabbage-size roll out of his briefcase to illustrate the bulk. Even the commissioners had to laugh at the thought of a man walking about, carrying such a wad.

When it was all over, Judge Forsyth said the manner in which Crockford had "conducted these transactions creates in me grave suspicion. The most charitable view that could be taken is that he has acted in a most imprudent manner."

Crockford was furious. When he came up for election that winter, he was trounced by a councillor, Gus Harris, a man, the reeve said, whose "association with leading communists is well known to everybody."

On election night, I wrote: "Tears in his eyes and a snarl in his voice, Reeve Oliver Crockford of Scarboro climbed into his big, brown Cadillac last night and drove out of public life." I've always been rather fond of it.

As the decade went by, the criminal bar grew but, in trial after trial, the same legendary band of advocates captured the headlines. Three years after the Dick case, Robinette was back in Hamilton over the killing at Irish Davey's bootlegging establishment. At Irish's place, a small frame house on the Lake Ontario shore near Hamilton, a man could place a small bet, buy a large drink or dip into the constantly bubbling Irish stew that gave the place its name.

As Jack Batten tells it, some young men burst into Irish's place one night, presumably bent on mayhem or money, and the bartender, Dempsey Richards, shot one of them. Sports-writer Jim Coleman, who had featured Irish Davey in a bunch of columns, rallied the defense and Robinette and Maloney were retained. Irish got off; Dempsey got manslaughter.

Robinette told Batten he remembers two amusing side-lights. In the Dick case, Robinette said the papers kept refer-ring to him as "the young counsel." In the Irish Davey case, he was a "veteran counsel": "I'd gone from youth to old age in two years.

"And when Arthur and I came to get paid, Jim Coleman arrived with the cash in the hotel room in Hamilton. He counted the piles of ones and twos and fives that Irish's customers had collected for the defense fund. They were loyal to Irish Davey, and Jim Coleman was the most loyal of all."

Reporters remember how Maloney over the years developed an affection for immigrants. He asked that he be buried in a Lithuanian cemetery near Toronto. And he seldom turned down a request for help if the accused was a frightened newcomer.

On one occasion, Maloney was defending an Albanian immigrant, a butcher, who had stabbed a man called Gafi in the neck when the two men met to discuss Gafi's interference in Maloney's client's home life.

"My client fell on the street, on the concrete, from a blow struck by Gafi," Maloney recalled. "It was a large blow, witnessed by other people. When he got up, he wandered around like a chicken without a head. He pulled his knife and stabbed Gafi in the back of his neck. Gafi died on the spot."

Why was Maloney's man carrying a knife? "He was carrying a knife because he was a butcher and he didn't want anyone else using the knife while he was away from the shop."

Maloney's successful defense, backed by an expert witness, was that the blow had made his client an automaton and he was not responsible for his actions. His client was acquitted all the way to the Supreme Court.

Dave Humphrey says some of the new criminal-bar lawyers, such as Eddie Greenspan, remind him of the fifties. "Greenspan has a fabulous sense of humor. Everything is not death or income taxes."

But the old watering holes where lawyers and reporters gathered—the Metropole, the Radio Artists Club, the Mercury—are long gone. And the new places, the Library Bar at the Royal York, the Advocates Club, Winstons, are too spiffy for guys defending winos, snowbirds and chickenhawks.

The legendary gunslingers of the criminal bar of the fifties —most of them dead now—would likely agree with Judge Louis D. Brandeis who has mused: "It is true that at the present time the lawyer does not hold that position with the people that he held fifty years ago, but the reason is not, in my opinion, lack of opportunity.

"It is because, instead of holding a position of independence between the wealthy and the people, prepared to curb the excesses of either, the able lawyers have to a great extent allowed themselves to become an adjunct of the great corporations and have neglected their obligations to use their powers for the protection of the people."

But what the hell, as Arthur Maloney would say when addressing the bar, let's have another drink.

9 The Miracle of Springhill

At 8:06 on an October evening, with a bump that jiggled the earthquake meters 100 miles away, the unimaginable weight of a mile-deep layer of rock and dirt collapsed a series of underground tunnels beneath the town of Springhill, Nova Scotia, where 174 miners dug for coal.

In an instant, dozens of men were crushed to death, dozens more mangled, many suffocated; a few, coughing and black, scrambled to safety. But in a number of chambers formed by some twisted configuration of rock and coal, men lived.

And that was to be the Miracle of Springhill.

By the time the last man was buried, the last woman comforted and the last of hundreds of newspaper, radio and television reporters left, there would be seventy-five miners dead. They died making $11 a day in a dying industry in a town where death was commonplace.

Since 1827 when Lodewick Hunter first began selling coal to blacksmiths in the town known for its number of springs, men had been killed digging out the glistening black stuff. Careful count had been kept, and from 1881, when the

Springhill Collieries began operation, until after the disaster on October 23, 1958, 424 men and boys had died underground.

A white marble monument, topped by a figure of a miner, stands in the center of the town of Springhill, a memorial to the 125 men who died in 1891, the first massive loss of life. As recently as 1956, an explosion had rocked the No. 4 Colliery of the Dominion Steel and Coal Corporation Ltd., taking the lives of 39 men.

Springhill is a comfortable town. Most of the miners owned their own homes in the fifties, drove newish cars, drank beer at the Miners' Hall and, once in a while, had a shopping weekend in Halifax.

The mine was the deepest in the world, nearly a mile below the surface, two miles down the slopes by rake, a man-carrying trolley that dropped the miners off at various levels, ending at the 13,000-foot wall. There, in the heat and dust, the men hammered at the coal seam with pneumatic picks and loaded the coal onto conveyor belts where it was transferred to boxes and hauled to the surface.

When the first news of the bump reached the newsroom in Toronto on Thursday, October 23, the obvious man for the *Tely* to send was night police reporter Bert Petlock. Petlock had been in Springhill in 1956 when mine officials had to seal off men trapped underground in an attempt to stop fires from spreading. It was a "heart-wrenching decision" Petlock had written then. But he was also able to report a day later that fifty-nine men had struggled out.

He left for Springhill, along with a team from the *Star*, and was able to report in Friday's paper that the death toll "threatened to mount to 93—the worst mining disaster in recent Canadian history."

Despite the developing story, key *Telegram* executives decided it was too nice a day in Toronto, sunny and warm, to stay in the office. They would play golf. It turned out to be a mistake.

After managing editor Doug MacFarlane, assistant managing editor Ted McCall, city editor Art Cole and chief police reporter Doug Creighton left for the Scarborough Golf Club, it became clear Petlock needed help fast. Someone was inspired to suggest the fastest way to get to Springhill would be by chartered plane, and who had a nice, big private aircraft but the publisher's friends, the Eaton family. The only man left on the desk, Doug Steubing, decided to call the publisher and ask him to ask the Eatons if the *Tely* could borrow their plane.

John Bassett agreed to try but suggested that Steubing check with MacFarlane first.

"Can't do that, sir," said Steubing, "he's not here at the moment."

"Well, get McCall," said Bassett. Same answer.

"Well, for Christ's sake, get me Art Cole."

"Sorry, sir, it's a golf game."

"You mean to tell me," screamed Bassett, "that on the day the biggest national story of the year is breaking, my entire executive is out playing golf?"

Out on the seventeenth green at the Scarborough club, a cheerful MacFarlane was teeing up for a long drive. A puffing messenger arrived from the clubhouse and insisted he come to the phone.

When MacFarlane got back, Creighton remembers, he was black with rage. "That was Bassett," he snarled, as he teed up his ball for a last swing. The ball soared 200 yards down the fairway. Creighton, awed, said, "My God, Doug, how did you do that?"

"I just pretended it was Steubing's head," said MacFarlane, picking up his bag to head back to the office.

The Eatons were happy to lend us their plane, after a call from Bassett, and a hastily assembled team—Dorothy Howarth, Phyllis Griffiths, Peter Ward and I—headed for the airport. At the Montreal airport, where we landed for fuel, the pilot spotted a distinguished woman waiting in the lounge. "Oh my God," he said, "it's Lady Eaton and we've got her airplane."

It didn't matter. She waved us on and we headed into the fog over Nova Scotia. Bert Petlock met us with rented cars, his own a giant black Cadillac—the last rental car, he claimed, available within a hundred miles of Springhill.

The *Star*'s team, including my colleagues from Canadian Press days in Vancouver, Ray Timson and veteran Ed Feeney, were already there, at the closest hotel, the Amherst Inn. They also had with them a free-lance photographer, Ron Laytner, who was to be a great help to the *Tely* in the following days.

At the minehead, in the drizzling rain and mud, the kerchiefed women waited for word. The Salvation Army had set up three huge tents, with tables, chairs and pot-bellied stoves. These were the meeting places. By the second day, 137 press people had rushed to Springhill to wallow in the mud and their own prose. One reporter, John Thompson from *The Dartmouth Free Press*, was killed when his car ran off the highway as he raced to the mine.

A mile beneath our feet—we learned from interviews later—living men crawled about in two lightless caverns.

Levi Milley, somersaulted through the air by the wind from the collapsing tunnels, lay panting in the darkness. He could hear groaning and screaming all about him.

A voice nearby said: "My damn leg is caught. Someone take the stone off my leg . . ."

Milley's miner's light still glowed from his cap and he crawled over and recognized Caleb Rushton. He rolled the stone off Caleb's leg, which did not seem to be broken. The two men crawled along, their stabbing lights illuminating bodies, wreckage, tools, shattered helmets and lamps. They came upon Joe McDonald, whose leg was pinned under a beam. "Jesus, don't leave me," he pleaded. Rushton and Milley assured him they weren't going anywhere.

Further on, Bowman Maddison lay in the darkness, his lamp cord severed by a flying piece of coal. The three of them, Maddison in the middle, continued to look for survivors. Young Larry Leadbetter was ten feet away. "My God, oh my God," he cried. "It was awful. Don't leave me alone here. Please. I don't want to die. I'm only twenty-two. I've got a wife and kids."

Maddison growled, "None of us want to die, dammit" and told him to be quiet.

Within an hour, there were twelve living men, huddling in the darkness to save their lamp batteries. They had found two quarts of water in dead men's cans and two devilled-ham sandwiches in a lunch box. Eldred Lowther had come up with an aspirin bottle that they could use to ration the water.

Caleb Rushton, who sang in the church choir, began softly to sing: "I fancy I stood by the shore one day, Of the beautiful murmuring sea; I saw the great crowds as they thronged the way . . . Of the Stranger of Galilee." Slowly the others joined him until they were all singing together in a tomb forty-three feet long and sixteen feet wide.

On the surface, the Draegermen had arrived.

These were Nova Scotia's legendary heroes, ordinary miners especially trained for the dangerous work of going below ground after a disaster wearing special breathing equipment invented by a German scientist, Alexander Bernhard Draeger. The pack weighed forty-five pounds. The Draegerman's first job was to provide safe breathing air in the mine, then to locate the injured and take them to safety.

Leonard Lerner of the Boston *Globe*, who covered both the 1956 and 1958 Springhill disasters, described their work. "The Draegerman hauled his equipment into the unknown, into rockfalls, broken timbers, gas. He crawled across jagged chunks of rock and coal, through narrow openings, scraping his shoulders and cutting his hands and knees, to reach men in trouble, men depending on him."

In the long, drizzly days at the pithead, when nothing seemed to be happening, we interviewed the Draegermen, prowled the mine buildings and interviewed wives, much of it tasteless, mawkish stuff. *Tely* and *Star* readers learned that the miners began each day at the washhouse, a long, rambling building where they changed into their workclothes. The clothes were in buckets suspended from the ceiling, raised and lowered by ropes. At the other end of the building were the showers, but the men said they never seemed to be able to get all the grime off. Before going down in the rake, each man handed his brass, numbered tag in exchange for a lamp. It was these tags, row upon row, that told how many men had not come up after the bump.

The funerals had begun and the papers pressed us for pictures and stories. It was a miserable job. The miners' families didn't want us at the cemeteries and were becoming weary of interviews. Ron Laytner of the *Star* was a help. He brashly crashed every funeral and was roundly despised by the families. So, each time one of the *Tely* men had to flee a cemetery, pushed out by the angry miners, he would shout over his shoulder: "I'm Ron Laytner of the *Star* and you can't do this to me." It saved our bacon and nobody much liked Laytner anyway.

(Timson was to encounter him later during the wood-workers' strike in Newfoundland where, fleeing angry wood-workers, Laytner pushed his way into a nunnery, yelling "Sanctuary, sanctuary." The Mother Superior, shocked that a man was inside her walls, shoved him out again.)

On Friday morning, Harold Gordon, Dosco's vice-president and general manager, told the company's public relations director, Arnie Patterson, that he'd better call a press conference. "I've got some bad news."

The press crowd was somber. Lerner recalls one reporter who told about finding a small boy wandering aimlessly around the mine grounds.

"What's the trouble, sonny?" he was asked.

"I'm looking for my daddy."

"Where is he?"

"He's in the mine. He hasn't come up yet."

The reporter, fighting tears, said, "Well, I think you'd better go home."

"No, no," the boy said. "I don't want to go home. Everybody's crying there."

Gordon arrived, his face still powdered with coal. He said, "I have just returned from the mine. I have bad news. There are no more men alive at the 13,000- and 13,800-foot levels. There are tremendous piles of debris at every entrance. For the men in there, there may be some hope. But I say that only because I haven't seen them. The way things look, those still listed as missing must be presumed dead. There is virtually no hope left. That is all I can tell you."

There were thirty-two known dead, ninety-three rescued and forty-nine missing.

But Gordon was wrong. There were men alive at the 13,000-foot level.

Four hundred feet away from where twelve men were entombed, more men were alive, one only barely. Garnet Clarke, Herb Pepperdine, and Currie Smith had survived the blast and they had managed to dig out Doug Jewkes, who had been covered in coal up to his waist. And there was Maurice Ruddick, the man who, more than any other, symbolized the courage and spirit of the miracle miners.

Ruddick was a mulatto, a handsome man with twelve children. He sang a rich baritone in a Springhill quartette. They called him the Singing Miner. The roof had fallen on Ruddick when the bump came, but he dug himself out and began to lurch along the passage. The foul air got him and he collapsed. When he regained consciousness, he heard someone calling "For Christ's sake, someone help me." It was Percy Rector, caught with his arm jammed into a pile of pit props. There were others with him. In the light from one lamp, Clarke wrote the names of the survivors on a piece of timber. There were seven.

Rector was in terrible pain but there was no way to free him. Ruddick found he had a box of aspirin in his pocket. He crawled over to Rector. "Here, try these. They'll help the pain." The trapped man swallowed three of them. After a while he dozed off. The men found a few cans of water and a couple of pieces of broken ham sandwich. Ruddick started to sing "I come to the Lord in prayer . . ." But he stopped. He said he didn't feel much like singing.

The twelve men, 400 feet away had started digging. But it was clear it was no use, so they stopped. They laughed when Levi Milley took off his boots, saying, "Well, I guess I'll stick around for a while." Then someone remembered the pipe. As the twelve later told their stories to Griffiths and Howarth, they started digging again, hoping to reach the six-inch pipe.

"We knew where it was. It was a section from which they would have to come to get us. We knew that if the other end was uncovered we had a chance. They might hear us pounding on it or yelling through it. We were lucky we had plenty of tools. We took turns until at last we dug out the pipe. We took turns banging on it or yelling down it. We made sure someone was always beside it."

Joe McDonald had a broken hip and it was swelling. He said it didn't hurt much unless he moved and then he could hear the bones grinding.

In Lerner's interviews with the men later, Milley recalled that at one point they realized it was Sunday.

"If we were home we'd be on our way to church. We can pray here." The men huddled and Caleb Rushton began his hymn. "Abide with me, fast falls the eventide . . ." The men knelt and Caleb Rushton offered a prayer.

"Dear God, you know the fix we're in. We don't know any way out of it. We haven't got any food and we're out of water. Please, God, save us and bring us back to our families. Every one of us has a wife and we've got kids, too. They need us and we need them."

The others whispered Amen.

On the surface, the days had become cold and windy. And boring. There was a lot of drinking. One *Star* man called me early in the morning and said he was in jail, could I raise some bail money. Sure, I said, how much? I heard him turn away from the phone and yell, "Hey warden, how much is bail? . . . Twenty-five dollars. Shit, why didn't you tell me. I've got twenty-five dollars." He hung up.

And some curious vultures were arriving. Public-relations people from Montreal and Toronto, offering blankets and toys for the kids and other junk for the miners' families. And maybe we would mention that the Gee Whiz Toy Company had donated the stuff. We were running out of interviews, out of funerals, the story was dying, time to go home. It was Tuesday now and Dosco general manager Harold Gordon, his face black and his eyes bloodshot, called another press conference. The digging crews were up against nearly solid rock and were making only about ten or twelve feet each shift.

"There is no further hope. There just can't be. We cannot hold any reason to believe that men will be found alive when we finally do reach them."

The men's families began slowly to leave the tents. They would wait at home for the final word.

In one of the crypts, Caleb Rushton remembered it was his son's second birthday. The men felt sad. "Then someone begins singing 'Happy Birthday to You' and we sing it over and over. And we sing hymns. The trouble with singing is that it makes you think of the time you sang at home or in church." They kept rapping on the pipe.

On the other side of the wall of rock and coal, there was a real birthday party. Garnet Clarke announced he was twenty-nine today—"the way it looks, I won't get a chance to get any older." Ruddock roused the others. "We're going to have a birthday party," he said. "We've got one sandwich left, so let's have it now. We'll have a real party and I'll get roaring drunk." The men nibbled the last of the sandwich and wet their lips with the last of the water. "Happy birthday, dear Garnie, happy birthday to you."

Percy Rector was screaming. "I can't stand it any more. Cut off the arm. I'm begging." Pepperdine found a saw. "It might kill him," one man said. "Why don't we vote?" They all voted no. Rector screamed again.

Over at the twelve's tomb, Bowman Maddison was crunching on a piece of coal. It didn't help much and it made him thirstier. One man pissed in a can and moistened his lips with it. They kept pounding the pipe.

It was 11:00 A.M. on Wednesday and rescue worker Earl Wood, digging at the 13,000-foot level, figured he had about sixty feet to go before reaching the coal-seam wall where the men had been working. Suddenly his pick hit metal—the end of a six-inch pipe. Wood smashed his pick into the wall and there was a whoosh as the debris gave way and a wave of dust and fetid air hit him. He scrambled back, fearing gas. Slowly the dust cleared. Chief surveyor Blair Phillips moved toward the pipe, his headlamp shining at the opening.

Back in the tomb, Harold Brine thought he caught a reflection. "It's a light," he whispered. "Yell into the pipe," the huddled men said. At the other end, a miracle. Phillips, bending close, couldn't believe his ears. He heard a voice through the pipe yelling: "There are twelve of us alive . . . for God's sake come and get us."

Up top, the news spread from the pithead through the town to the press tent. Everyone raced for the phones and then to the pithead. Twelve men were still alive. It was a sensation.

Down below Phillips yelled through the pipe, "Your names. Give us your names." Gorley Kempt called them out—Harold Brine . . . Joe McDonald . . . Caleb Rushton . . . Larry Leadbetter . . . Hughie Guthro . . . Tiddy Michniak . . .— one after another, clearly and proudly. Phillips memorized each one and raced for the surface. The town came alive as phones began to ring in a dozen houses.

One of the first men below when communications were established was Dr. Arnold Burden from All Saints Hospital in Springhill. As soon as he got back to the surface I grabbed him for an interview and quickly wrote an "As told to" story.

"Our feeding system was pretty makeshift but it worked perfectly from the beginning. The pipe was too big to pour things down so we tried shoving a plastic tube through. It was too short. We tried a copper tube next but it was still too short. Then I sent up top and had a 60-foot copper tube sent down. We pushed it through the pipe and the men got a hold of it at the other end.

"Meanwhile, up top someone had been sent to Amherst for a spraying pump. He came back with a tree-sprayer from an Amherst hardware store. He hooked it up to the copper tube, filled it with water and started pumping. I told the men they could have one mouthful of water at a time, count 500 and have another. At the other end, the men caught the water in their lunchboxes and an empty water can.

"After a while, we started to send along hot, sweet coffee and no milk and gradually stepped up the amounts a man could have."

At noon, Dr. Burden yelled down the pipe, "How would you fellows like some soup?"

"What kind?" Kemp joked.

"This is no restaurant," the doctor said. "Tomato soup. Take it or leave it."

"We'll take it, we'll take it," said Kemp. "I was only kidding."

One of the men yelled to the Draegerman, shovelling through the rubble, "Hurry up. I've got to get home and feed the chickens. I think I'm going to get out of the mining business and get into the chicken business." The last they got was soup spiked with Vitamin A and ascorbic acid. The first thing they asked for when the wall finally crumbled was cigarettes.

All Saints Hospital was bedlam when the rescued men began arriving. Hundreds of press waited until they were settled and then we were let in, a few at a time. We raced from bed to bed, shouting questions.

The rescued men had each lost ten pounds, but seemed not

to have suffered ill effects from munching coal and sipping urine. Zora Maddison, Bowman's daughter, stood at the foot of his bed. She stared at him. She had not left the pithead since word had reached her that men were alive in the mine. Tears poured down her cheeks. Then she ran to her father's side, sobbing, "Oh Daddy, Daddy, I love you so." In Toronto, we were close to deadline and it was a nice question how much time to spend listening and how much time it would take to phone.

My Page One lead read: "They were bearded and dirty and they smeared the hospital sheets with coal dust. When they spoke, it was with bloody tongues and cracked lips. They looked like what they were—12 men who should have been dead, but lived to be hauled out of the pitch-black tomb."

For the *Star*, Timson wrote: "Six days of hymns and humor helped keep 12 tough miners' hopes alive so the 'miracle of Springhill' could happen. Roman Catholic and Protestant, they sang hymns together. They punctuated the hymns with Keystone cop-type humor."

It was an exhilarating moment. A tremendous, good-news story. A kind of professional calm settles as you dictate from scribbled notes. I had the best rewrite man in the business, Jim Foster, steady, fast, always ready if I couldn't find a word.

Reporters left the hospital, drying their eyes. The *Tely* was on the phone when I got back to the hotel. Royalty was coming.

A mile below ground and 400 feet from where the twelve men were found The Seven heard nothing. They were barely alive. But the Singing Miner still felt strong. He was writing a song for when he was rescued:

The twenty-third of October, we'll remember that day,
Down the shaft underground in our usual way . . .

[something like that . . .]
In the Cumberland pit town, the rafters crash down
And black hell closed around us, way down in the
ground . . .

Not bad, sung slow.

Garnet Clarke stared at the bark on the pit props. He'd read somewhere about guys keeping alive chewing bark. He stripped a piece off, dipped it in urine and chewed. It tasted awful, but it stayed down.

Ruddick noticed that Percy Rector's body was feeling awfully cool, considering it was so hot in the pit. Rector breathed in, then out, and died.

The editor on the phone from Toronto said, "Prince Philip is in Canada on some Commonwealth thing and he's going to stop off in Springhill and give the miners a boost. Go find out what they think."

Oh shit, I thought, I know what they'd think. Not much. How will I handle the looks when I ask that question?

I drove to the pithead. It was dark, drizzling, mud everywhere as usual. I waited until a shift of Draegermen came to the surface. I walked after one man who was slumped with weariness, his face black and covered with welts from his mask. I tapped him on the shoulder.

"Excuse me, sir," I said, "I'm from the Toronto *Telegram*. Prince Philip is coming to Springhill tomorrow to give you guys a boost. What do you think of that?"

He stopped. Turned around and looked at me and said: "Kinda tall for this close work, ain't he?"

Philip arrived on Friday, October 31, and immediately went to the hospital to talk to the rescued men. On his way, as his limo paused by the washhouse, a miner yanked open the door and invited the prince in for a look. "Not on the schedule," he smiled and closed the door again. At the hospital, Philip broke all royal protocol by signing George Hayden's cast.

The people of Springhill lined the main street to see him. But it was bizarre for it was Hallowe'en and the children—too young to appreciate tragedy—were painted and masked and sheeted. The little ghosts waved at the prince.

Philip told Caleb Rushton that he had met a man once who had wintered in a snow cave in the Arctic and found that singing helped. "I think it might help the nerves," said Caleb.

He asked Ken Gilbert how he felt. "Fine," snapped Gilbert, "how's yourself?" Philip looked startled and replied, "Oh, I'm fine, thank you."

Joe McDonald's leg was in traction and he had a tube feeding in his arm but he was grinning at the prince. "You had a long wait underground," Philip said.

"Yes. We all did. From now on I want the sky for my roof."

Out at the tents, it was getting dark as Philip, tall in his black coat, stepped around the ropes. I lost him and said to the man in front of me "Where is the big sonovabitch?"

"The big sonovabitch is right in front of you," said Prince Philip, turning around, unsmiling.

Philip asked Harold Gordon if it was possible any more were still alive.

"I hardly think so," Gordon said. The prince shook his head.

When Prince Philip had gone, the story was surely over. Gordon was asked at a press conference whether a man could live eight or nine days without food or water. "No," Gordon said.

With the water all gone, Currie Smith was sipping on oil from a wrecked machine. Doug Jewkes was afraid of the rats. "We could hear them. We were afraid they would eat us." Once they heard the noise of a pick and everyone began to scream. Then the noise stopped. And there was nothing.

"When do you think we'll die?" Garnet Clarke asked. "Soon, I hope," Smith said. "I can't take any more. I wish it happened right away. Why does it have to take so long?"

Maurice Ruddick, determined not to give up hope, began singing again: "Rock of Ages, cleft for me, Let me hide myself in Thee . . ."

Byron Martin was delirious. His fingers were bloody from scratching the rock.

At the Amherst Inn we were having a party.

Arnie Patterson of Dosco had arranged it. The company was now certain there was no one left alive and, before the press left, they wanted to thank them for what had been, in the circumstances, quite reasonable cooperation.

We drank and danced and ate and drank some more. Early in the morning, I staggered back to my room and climbed into bed. I was well in the bag. A few minutes after I'd turned the light out, the door was flung open. There was Phyl Griffiths in her bathrobe. She was shouting at me. "Val, hurry up, get up. They've found more miners alive . . ."

I sat up thinking, my goodness, that's a helluva story. I must get on that first thing in the morning, and slumped back on the pillow. Ten seconds later, prompted by some curious, still-operating brain circuitry, I sat up again . . . What did she say?

Minutes later, with Petlock at the wheel, our big, black Cadillac was heading back to Springhill.

A few hours earlier, below ground, the dying seven had found a narrow pipe and were banging on it from time to time with a tin cup. Not far away, Harold Gordon was flat on his stomach. He was filling a bucket with dirt and rock and passing it back. As the rescue forces had discovered much earlier, getting rid of the rubble was a real problem. There was nowhere to put the dug-out earth except behind them, the way they came in. So it took a long line of men to move the buckets. Gordon kept hacking at the wall with a short-handled pick. He uncovered a section of pipe. "We're going in the right direction," he said.

Ahead of them Currie Smith continued to hit the pipe . . . tap . . . tap, tap . . . tap. But he was growing so weak, he could hardly keep the tin cup moving.

Then, at 4:45 A.M. at the other end of the pipe, they heard it. Tap . . . tap . . . tap. Matt Pearson heard it first and shouted, "Hear that, there's someone alive." Bill Downey crawled backwards and headed for the emergency phone. Later, he told reporter Lerner that he seemed to wait for hours. Then a voice answered, "Yes, hello." Downey was too choked to speak. Then "we heard tappings on the pipe. There was someone alive down there."

It took the crew nearly an hour to break through the last twelve feet of rock and coal. They plunged through the last hole . . . and stumbled over the still-breathing body of Byron Martin. Martin, his fingers bloody, somehow managed to smile. "God must have saved this little hole for me. Thank God I'm alive . . . I didn't think anything could be so bad."

Jim Rossong swung his light around. There was Maurice Ruddick sitting on a rock and grinning. "Give me a drink and I'll sing you a song," the Singing Miner said.

Reporters raced around to the survivors' houses as soon as the names were known.

Ruddick's wife said she was in bed when there was a knock on the door.

"I'd been so scared to think of the minister coming. When I heard the knock I asked my sister to answer it. The minister came in and told me Maurice was saved. I grabbed him and hugged him. I still don't know quite what I'm doing."

Currie Smith's wife, Mabel, just leaned on the fridge and cried and cried.

It was over.

Roger David Brown, who taught school at Southampton, a village eight miles from Springhill, wrote a slim little pamphlet about Springhill's tragedies many years later.

At the end, he said:

> The number two mine never reopened. Hard times came to Springhill. People, hard pressed, went to the great slag heap to gather fuel for themselves. Some lit fires, which burned among the piles of coal and after a while proved impossible to put out. Near the present [Miners] museum these acres of coal can be seen and smelled burning. The government estimated it would cost a million dollars to put out the fire.
>
> The pollution of the town dropped to the five thousand level, little more than it had been in 1891. In 1970 the mine closed. That was the end of mining in Springhill.

But, in fact, the federal government ordered a prison to be built there. And a battery manufacturer opened a factory.

Now, at the end of the eighties, few Canadians think of Springhill as the place where the mine collapsed and seventy-five men died. They think of singer Anne Murray. She was born there.

The *Star* and the *Tely* had thrown massive resources into the Springhill story but it was easier for the *Star*. "We had the money to spend and the *Tely* didn't," Harry Hindmarsh said.

The decade was approaching its end with the *Tely* circulation at the time of Springhill at 214,437. The *Star* was publishing 308,340 from Monday to Saturday in the same period.

But Bassett that year was still having a wonderful time with the paper. He toured Italy, Israel and London writing Page One pieces on the economic and political state of each nation.

As his biographer, Maggie Siggins, wrote, "the only dark shadow during these happy years was the death of John Bassett Senior on 12 February 1958. Bassett Senior had given his son one invaluable piece of advice: a publisher's job was full time.

"Bassett was developing other interests, primarily in the sports field. After his father's death he began to branch out in several directions. Many people thought it was the beginning of the end of *The Telegram*."

Today, Bassett says no. Everything he was doing outside the *Tely* was to support the *Tely*.

"I tried to find other means to generate revenue. I bought all the property I could around the old *Tely* building. I thought, Jeez, I'll get into development business. I sold the land for $3 million. I bought Maple Leaf Gardens shares for $800,000. They bought me out for $5 million. We had thrown all that profit in."

But the Golden Decade was dimming. *The Telegram* would go on publishing. The sixties wasn't the end. But you could see it from there.

10 | The Post-Warriors

No one shouts for rewrite anymore. One by one, the country's newsrooms became sober and silent in the decades after the fifties, the only sound the click of computers and the occasional gurgle of Perrier into an editor's glass. Some papers were deathly quiet, killed by their owners, newspaper chains run by bookkeepers. The wars were over.

Ian Gill, a reporter on the Vancouver *Sun*, once a match for the *Star* and *Tely* as a cheeky, frolicsome, readable paper for over a century, describes *The Sun* newsroom today: "Walk in, right on deadline and listen. You will not hear the clack of ideas and opinions banging together. Nor will you hear the manic cackle of a newsman relishing a paragraph he just knows is going to stop 'em dead downtown. There is no edge to the place, no creative tension. No one dresses outrageously, no one argues out loud. It is more like a merchant bank than a newsroom."

What happened was television.

Newspapers, an editor once remarked, are not in the business of selling news any more than Black and Decker is in the business of selling drills. Black and Decker is selling holes. The papers are selling information. And if somebody figures out a better way of packaging information than a newspaper, the papers are in trouble.

Television found a better way. It was more exciting, more compelling, easier to absorb. As the decade of the fifties came to a close, the papers tried frantically to match television's power both as a storyteller and as a medium able to deliver news as a quick hit. Not only did many of the publishers fail, but the money and glamor of television began to draw good reporters away from the papers. Jack Webster left *The Sun*; Knowlton Nash, United Press and *The Financial Post*; Bruce Phillips, Southam; Peter Trueman, the *Tely*.

A whole new breed of paper entrepreneurs arrived—the newspaper consultants. They were to transform newspapers into print television, add a Lifestyle, Trend, Thank God It's Friday section. And tailor the news to new generations of people in a hurry.

Some editors resisted. In one Halifax newsroom, a consultant arrived to pep up the place, make it more relevant. He called the editor and said: "You people have problems and I'm here to deal with them. First, your staff—I want a rundown of age, experience, length of service, broken down by sex."

"Oh, we're not broken down by sex," replied the editor, gravely. "Booze is our problem."

In Toronto, the *Tely* scrambled frantically to stay alive.

There were a few laughs left . . . like the Great Lindsay Bullfight, the funniest story I ever covered. It was, as the lead said, "the goldarndest bullfight that ever was."

"Before it was over," I wrote, "a lady matador was in hysterics; the chief of police had lost his hat, his dignity and his clip-on bow tie after zigging instead of zagging when the bull charged; a pair of extremely capable Mexican matadors had vowed never to leave their country again; and several members of the Lindsay Chamber of Commerce were left sitting in a corner of the stands, moaning softly and steadily."

It seemed to the Chamber of Commerce a good idea at the time: stage a bullfight for the Lindsay Fall Fair but, for goodness sake, let's not really kill the bull. And that was the rub.

The first bull was released, ambled into the plywood stadium, took one look at the imported matador, Jorge Luis Bernal, in his pink suit of lights, and fled to the farthest corner of the ring, the matador flapping after him. "Chicken," yelled the crowd. "Hamburger."

A Zorro-like character galloped in, swinging a lariat. That was the absolute end for Ferdinand. He took off around the ring and while the band played martial music, round and round Zorro and the bull galloped and the crowd cheered. The two matadors just stood there staring, struck dumb by the spectacle.

Finally, the bull spotted the chute and plunged in. Time for the second bull, a lively critter upon whom the matadors could practice their cape arts.

But then the problem: how to get a live bull out of the ring. The Moment of Truth hadn't arrived; there would be no Death in the Afternoon.

For forty-five minutes the bull was shooed and pushed. Nothing. Finally a seductive heifer was led in to entice Ferdie outside for goodness knows what delights. The bull wasn't having any. She mooed invitingly. He turned away.

But, wait, Chief John L. Hunter, a mighty man, leaped over the fence with a rope in his hand. The bull charged. Hunter got it right in the midriff. His clip-on tie soared off and down he went, unhurt. I was laughing so hard, I could barely lift my camera but did manage to get a marvelous five-column picture of the hit that is still one of my favorites.

Humane Society officials were concerned about the "mental anxiety" of the bull as the chief limped off.

When the afternoon finally wore out, it had been a comic triumph—for everyone but the matadors, the bulls and the Chamber of Commerce.

It was almost the last story I wrote for the *Tely*. The sixties were beginning, television had arrived and I had a new trade to learn—political journalism—at the *Star*.

For ten years and more in Ottawa and London and Washington I thumped away, spending the *Star*'s money in grand style, wandering about the world and, whenever I could, writing features.

Like most newspaper and magazine writers I was captured by the New Journalism of the seventies.

It began in *The New York Herald Tribune* and later *New York* magazine. It was an exciting way of telling stories by piling detail upon detail, by adding personal feelings, especially the addled insights of the drug culture, and by burrowing under the skin of bikers, hookers, car customizers, political organizers until you could pop them out of the page, they seemed so real.

Newspaper storytellers didn't have the time, money or space to do anything but a model of the big magazine or book works. But we tried to imitate Tom Wolfe, Truman Capote, Hunter S. Thompson, Terry Southern, Joan Didion and Gary Wills.

In some of their work, fact melted into fiction, a temptation we were supposed to resist and usually did. Unhappily, some of us got caught when we failed. Janet Cook of *The Washington Post* had to give up her Pulitzer prize when it was discovered the black child she wrote about so poignantly was a composite—a favorite New Journalism technique—and not a real person. Composites were supposed to be so identified.

But the New Journalists' prose was impossible to ignore. Who could resist Wolfe's lead consisting entirely of a prolonged shriek from the window of a women's prison in New York City. Or Dr. Thompson's gonzo day at the Kentucky Derby where he and cartoonist Ralph Steadman had gone to report for a magazine.

"Steadman wanted to see some Kentucky colonels but he wasn't sure what they looked like," Thompson wrote. "I told him to go back to the clubhouse men's room and look for men in white linen suits vomiting in the urinals. 'They'll usually have large brown whiskey stains on the fronts of their shirts,' I said. 'But watch their shoes, that's the tipoff. Most of them manage to avoid vomiting on their own clothes, but they never miss their shoes.'"

I wrote a lead during that period about a sex clinic that began: "Sex, sex, sex, sex, sex, sex, sex, sex, sex, sex, sex, sex, sex, sex, sex, sex, sex. . . .

"Gotcha."

The editors loved it. But they didn't run it.

The New Journalism gradually wore out. Dr. Thompson became a sometime lecturer, the *New York Tribune* folded, *Rolling Stone* drifted into routine reporting.

Politics, as it turned out, lent itself admirably to storytelling. Where else can you find such a mix of greed, power, lust, conspiracy, sacrifice and secrecy?

There is a growing school of critics who argue the media has no business looking under the covers at a public man's private life. It is argued, with some logic, that if we were to elect only the blameless, our legislative halls would be filled with born-again Christians, nuns, and those of such overwhelming banality that government would die of ennui.

That is a danger. And yet I came to believe the press has business in the bedrooms of the political establishment. What a man is doing to his mistress at night, he is likely to do to the country in the morning. And for the same reason—for personal satisfaction.

I cannot believe, for instance, that Prime Minister Brian Mulroney's boyhood in Baie-Comeau and then in the boozing, battling, dallying, tall-story-telling Montreal legal community in the fifties is unrelated to his reputation for exaggeration.

Nor is it possible to form a proper assessment of Liberal leader John Turner until someone writes of his unswerving Roman Catholicism, explains that he reads his Bible every night, and tells that he drinks Scotch by the tumbler in private. It is useful to know that he can tell a woman journalist that he figures her shoes have been under a lot of beds and be surprised when she is offended, and that he is a driven man, with a holy fear of failure.

New Democratic Party leader Ed Broadbent, all soft-eyes and sincerity, was formed, it is helpful to know, out of a tough childhood with a difficult father. It is informative that his first marriage to a Japanese-Canadian woman failed, that he loves ethnic dancing and fast cars and has a remarkable talent for compromise.

The reporting of those intimate glimpses, those human insights, those unadmitted weaknesses and concealed strengths, adds a dimension to the otherwise cardboard men and women on the platform.

Without those glimpses we are compelled to make our judgments of public men based on a laundered record, a television clip or on who can afford the best speechwriter.

For the past twenty years, since leaving the *Tely*, I have been reporting about power, about politicians, about people.

I know the Davey Commission on the Media concluded the test for a good newspaper was how well it prepared its readers for social change. But someone has to grab them with a story first.

So while the Halifax *Chronicle-Herald* properly fills its pages with news of the plight of the navy, *The Gazette* exposes hospital expense accounts, *The Calgary Herald* reveals that some athletes are pumping drugs rather than iron and *The Vancouver Sun* turns inward and becomes what author Jan Morris called "the most boring newspaper in the world," we feature writers continue to prospect for the anecdotes that will save the newspaper-reading world from the boredom of death and economics.

The lives of the party leaders have always proved a rich lode.

Ed and Lucille Broadbent, a nice, *Saturday Evening Post* couple, were in Warsaw a few years back.

The day's carefully supervised work over, Ed asked their government guide and interpreter if they might go partying that evening.

The guide was enthusiastic but the security man was grumpy. Anyway, off they went, bar to bar, singing, dancing, sipping until the security man, zonked, slid under the table.

Then, the guide had an inspiration. He had a friend with a fire truck. Would his good friends, Ed and Lucille, like to see Warsaw at night by fire truck?

Of course. So off they went, slightly potted, careening around the Warsaw streets in the red wagon, having a helluva time.

The next morning, asked officially how the evening had gone, Ed replied: "Oh, very pleasant. Quiet, mind you, but pleasant."

Or imagine Flora MacDonald, once the dignified Secretary of State for External Affairs in the Clark government and later Minister of Communications for Mulroney, in New Delhi at midnight on Christmas eve.

Somehow she found a Presbyterian church for the midnight service. Leaving, alone, to walk back to her hotel, she was approached by a man on a motorcycle.

"Like a ride?" he said. "Sure," said Flora and climbed on the back.

They swooped around the city, having a wonderful time, until he delivered her safely to her lodging.

Isn't that a different Flora from Question Period, but still the finest woman ever to walk the streets of Kingston?

John Turner, as leader of the opposition, had a voice coach whose name was John Cromor. His theatrical colleagues called him Dr. Death because of his doom-laden voice and the fact he used to be a television medical reporter. Turner's Liberal friends called him Merlin because they say he transformed Turner's speaking style magically.

What Merlin decided was wrong with Turner—his staccato voice, his upflung arms, his bulging eyes—was that, in moments of stress, Turner's brain was telling him he wasn't breathing. That he was dying.

So several mornings a week, in his parliamentary office with the door locked, Turner shed his dignity, along with this coat and shoes, lay down on the floor and practised breathing.

That's as revealing about his dedication as his views on free trade.

Mulroney, of course, is almost too easy. You can write a whole book about rumors and truth and never need untangle the two.

We love to read he is a short-wave nut, preferring to listen to the politics abroad than the nastiness at home. Or that he has a small loudspeaker under his pillow so he can listen, without disturbing Mila.

It's great—and revealing—to sit down with old friends of his and listen to their yarns.

Like the time Bones was a bachelor lawyer in Montreal and was pursuing a quartette called the Gold-diggers. He'd dated three but the last was tough. He took the afternoon off from his law firm in hot pursuit. His boss, made privy to his designs during Mulroney's absence, left a note on Brian's desk beginning: "If you've finished your mining activities, I wonder if . . ."

Or the time he was walking out with an Italian girl and a friend, using a Mafia-godfather voice, warned him that he was about to be maimed. Mulroney fled to Baie-Comeau and stayed there until his friends phoned and said, Come back, Bones, it's a joke.

Or even the trip he took to Hungary as president of Iron Ore and was so pissed most of the time he could hardly remember what happened. That, and Mila, was what persuaded him to stop drinking for good. And stop smoking, too. Both evidence of the kind of determination and courage that help in making any political assessment.

Sometimes the politicians win.

Once the CBC's Mike Duffy, the only man to occupy two places in a *Chatelaine* poll of Canada's ten sexiest men, was testing a voice feed from the prairies to Ottawa. Told he had four minutes to fill instead of the two he had expected, Duffy said: "I'll have to put a lot of bullshit in."

Up in Harrington Lake, the prime minister's summer residence north of Ottawa, Mulroney had installed a television dish. The dish picked up Duffy's voice and the bullshit. Mulroney thought it was hilarious and dispatched an aide to tell Duffy the next day that he'd heard and agreed.

Duffy was aghast, ordering a double chocolate mousse to recover.

The backfence stories turned out to be the stuff of the eighties, as the New Journalism identified the seventies, up-beat "Living" stories the sixties and competitive razzle-dazzle the fifties.

The *Tely* began to die in the sixties when Bassett lost interest, and the *Star*, unstoppable, rolled over its rival.

In 1969, Bassett had fired his general, Doug MacFarlane, claiming he had "run out of steam." It was a cruel move. "John," MacFarlane said, "I'm only fifty-three years old. Why are you doing this?"

But Bassett was adamant. MacFarlane had to go, although he eased the pain with a $25,000-a-year pension.

The *Tely* had made its last profit in 1968 but it kept on publishing the way a dead man's fingernails keep on growing. And from time to time, Bassett would come into the editorial room and say: "This paper is not for sale, not in my lifetime, not in my sons' lifetimes and hopefully not in my grandson's lifetime."

Two years later it was dead.

Bassett, after dangling the *Tely*'s circulation list in front of the *Globe*, finally sold it to Beland Honderich of the *Star* for ten million dollars.

While the *Tely* was almost the first of the big post-war papers to go, the others were not far behind. In city after city, competition died and the survivors' profits rose. In one devastating day—August 27, 1980—both *The Ottawa Journal* and *The Winnipeg Tribune* were closed.

As competition ended, so did the battling journalism of the fifties wither. Blood, violence and crime disappeared from the headlines, to be replaced by politics, the disease of the week, "human" stories and local boosterism.

The perfect *Sun* story, jokes reporter Gill, would be "an interview with an AIDS-afflicted, wheel-chair bound pit-bull terrier planning a cross-country crawl to pay for an organ transplant."

Newsrooms, in the memorable words of the Davey Commission on Newspapers, became "boneyards of broken dreams."

There is no better illustration of the hunger in Canada's smaller cities and towns for good stories, well-told, than the success in the sixties of the television public-affairs show *This Hour Has Seven Days*. Despite its faults and television trickery, it was immensely popular as people without proper newspapers realized what a joy innovative, investigative reporting and storytelling could be.

New, journalism-school-trained reporters and editors began to move in and the roughnecks of the fifties and sixties had to change or get out. Some of "the terrible men," according to Heather Robertson of the old *Winnipeg Tribune*, did change. In Walter Stewart's book, *Canadian Newspapers*, she wrote: "They've dried out. They drink Perrier water. They've lost weight. They jog. They've quit smoking. They ski. They write books. They don't screw around. Some have found God. Some have found Joe Clark."

And some plainly rebelled. On *The Globe and Mail*, veteran photographer Harry Boyd was told by a wet, young night editor to hurry out and cover a suicide, a man had jumped off the Bloor Street viaduct. Boyd protested that the *Globe* didn't run suicides.

"Don't talk back to me, Boyd," yelled the editor. "Get the hell out there and get something."

Boyd drove to the viaduct and photographed the crumpled corpse. On the way back he stopped into a Chinese restaurant and begged a bag of chicken guts. In the *Globe* newsroom, he dumped the bloody mess on the editor's desk.

"That's all I could get," he said. "The *Star* got the rest."

The day the *Tely* died, a new paper was born, *The Toronto Sun*. It was founded by soldiers in the *Star* and *Tely* wars and it rose from the rubble of the Old Lady of Melinda Street to become an immensely successful, immensely profitable news-paper of the New Age.

If it is, as its critics complain, "junk journalism," it is the kind of junk that terrifies other publishers and satisfies a re-cord number of readers.

The *Sun* is largely the invention of Doug Creighton, an amiable, red-headed newsman who moved steadily upward on the *Tely* from police reporter to the city desk, to sports editor and, finally, in the *Tely*'s last days, to managing editor.

It was launched on November 1, 1971 from an old rented building, The Eclipse, across from Farb's Car Wash.

What some fifty-five ex-*Tely* people were publishing was a right-wing, tits-and-ass tabloid with plenty of sports and a new kind of personal journalism. Everything was to be kept short, the layout was flashy and the editorials would have all the subtlety of a steel-toed boot. On Page Three each day there would be a Sunshine Girl, a fleshy popsy of which To-ronto appeared to have a surfeit.

From the moment it first appeared, it was a success.

Creighton counted on an initial press run of 50,000 copies. The first day's run hit 75,000 and was a sellout. The next day 124,600 were sold.

In an early editorial, Worthington wrote: "One thing the *Sun* is not is a smaller edition of the *Telegram*. We are our-selves and political and fringe groups better believe it."

Did Creighton bring anything he learned at the *Tely* to the *Sun*?

"Shit, yes," he said recently. "You can't let the expenses go crazy. You've got to have the editorial product. But I think the palmy days of the *Sun* in terms of editorial product were the initial days. The palmy days in financial terms are the present days. I really do think it was at the *Tely* that the idea of very personal journalism developed."

Senator Keith Davey, who had once run a commission on newspapers, said he believed even the most determined right-wingers deserved a paper of their own. "And now, in *The Toronto Sun*, they've got it. The paper's so bad it actually makes Doug Fisher look like James Reston."

Nuts to that, says Creighton. "Ninety-five percent of the criticism that's leveled at the *Sun* comes from various other members of the media. If we were putting out a paper to satisfy them, we'd never have hit 100,000 circulation. We're putting out a paper to satisfy what we feel is our constituency."

Today, the *Sun* is into the kind of battle the old *Tely* relished, a new kind of newspaper war, just as bloody as the one in the fifties, just as fatal for the losers. Thirty years after the Marilyn Bell swim, Fabian of the Yard, Springhill and the Boyd Gang, newspapers in major cities are at one another's throats again.

In Halifax-Dartmouth, the tabloid *Daily News* has taken on the flabby old *Chronicle-Herald*, perhaps the worst newspaper in Canada. In Montreal, publisher Pierre Peladeau has invested $25 million in a new tabloid and the *Gazette* has added a Sunday edition. In Ottawa, a new tabloid, the *Herald*, is getting underway.

But it is in Toronto again where the battle smoke is thickest, the stakes highest and the war most costly. This time there are no disasters, no bullets and gore. The subject is money.

The *Sun*, through *The Financial Post*, and *The Globe and Mail* are the *Tely* and the *Star* of the eighties. And again, one may die. Although, this decade, we are not talking about a couple of family-owned firms with millions to play with. We are talking conglomerates and billions. Thomson Newspapers Ltd., with projected revenues of $1.4 billion this year, owns the *Globe*. While behind the *Post* is the *Sun*, which should earn $377 million in 1988. The *Sun*, in turn, is 60.5 percent owned by MacLean Hunter Ltd., a $1.3-billion publishing giant.

When the *Sun* announced it had purchased the *Post*, the editor of the *Post*, John Godfrey, said, "Our T and A will be Titles and Acquisitions."

The *Globe*, which has had a heavy hold on business readers through its *Report on Business*, is being challenged by the *Post*, which has gone daily from years as a successful weekly. And to add to the mix is the weekly *Financial Times*, a bustling financial tabloid, owned by the media giant Southam and the mighty *Toronto Star*, no slouch in the business department.

Some Bay Street people think the *Globe* is more likely to win the new war for the same reason the *Star* won the old —Thomson's have more money. But Creighton has another ace in the hole. He's in partnership with Conrad Black, who owns forty-four papers, including the *London Daily Telegraph*, and has more bread than a bakery. "I don't see running out of money as a problem for either us or the *Globe*," said Creighton.

Maclean's, reporting on the new war, said it "promises to be far less dramatic than attempting to kidnap Marilyn Bell, but both events are expressions of a common impulse in the newspaper business: the war for readers and revenue."

What newspapers discovered in the seventies and eighties that has revived them is technology—computers that can translate copy almost directly into type, eliminating hundreds of composing-room jobs. They have made newsrooms eerie places, carpeted and quiet, efficient and drear.

Editor Robert Fulford says the "environment in which journalists must function and develop and exercise their own rough versions of moral philosophy, is the corporate world of centralization, rationalization and minutely calculated expenditures."

No one, like John Bassett once did, runs a newspaper for fun any more.

But there are still editors and reporters, as Heather Robertson wrote in *Canadian Newspapers*, "scattered across the country, ornery as ever, noses twitching at the scent of bullshit, stubborn, smart, rude, still fighting after all these years."

And even when newspapers are not papers at all but a glow on the wall or a ribbon pouring out of a slot, they will still have a certain magic, brewed by men and women of a special kind.

The storytellers.

Here's to them.